INCOGNEGRO™
A GRAPHIC MYSTERY

AN IMPRINT OF
DARK HORSE COMICS

Story
MAT JOHNSON
Art
WARREN PLEECE
Letters
CLEM ROBINS

INCOG

Logo & Book Design
RICHARD BRUNING

NEGRO

A GRAPHIC MYSTERY

Editor
KAREN BERGER
Original Editor
JONATHAN VANKIN
Associate Editor
CARDNER CLARK
Digital Art Technician
CARY GRAZZINI
President & Publisher
MIKE RICHARDSON

Author's Note

I grew up a black boy who looked white.

This was in a predominantly African-American neighborhood, during the height of the Black Power era, so I stood out a bit. My mom even got me a dashiki so I could fit in with the other kids, but the contrast between the colorful African garb and my nearly blond, straight brown hair just made things worse. Along with my cousin (half black/half Jewish) I started fantasizing about living in another time, another situation, where my ethnic appearance would be an asset instead of a burden. We would "go incognegro," we told ourselves as we ran around, pretending to be race spies in the war against white supremacy.

I forgot my "incognegro" dreams until college, when I read about Walter White, the former head of the NAACP. White was an African-American even paler than I was. In the early 20th century, White went undercover, posing as a white man in the deep south to investigate lynchings. It was as if my little childhood fantasy had come to life. From then on, the idea continued to gestate. I started feeling that what once seemed silly was turning into something I had to write about.

The birth of my twins in 2005, one of whom is brown-skinned with black Afro hair, the other with the palest of pink skins and more European curly hair, brought the rest of the story home to me. Two people with the exact same ethnic lineage destined to be viewed differently only because of genetic randomness. From there, the story found itself.

And now it finds you.

— Mat Johnson

INCOGNEGRO: A GRAPHIC MYSTERY

10th Anniversary Edition: February 2018
ISBN 978-1-50670-564-4
1 0 9 8 7 6 5 4 3
Printed in China

Library of Congress Cataloging-in-Publication Data
Names: Johnson, Mat, author. | Pleece, Warren, artist. | Robins, Clem, letterer.
Title: Incognegro : a graphic mystery / written by Mat Johnson; art by Warren Pleece; lettered by Clem Robins; cover art by Warren Pleece.
Description: 10th anniversary edition. | Milwaukie, OR : Dark Horse Books, 2018. | Includes bibliographical references and index.
Identifiers: LCCN 2017037933 | ISBN 9781506705644 (hardback)
Subjects: LCSH: African Americans–Southern States–Comic books, strips, etc. | Passing (Identity)–Comic books, strips, etc. | Graphic novels. | BISAC: COMICS & GRAPHIC NOVELS / Literary. | COMICS & GRAPHIC NOVELS / Crime & Mystery
Classification: LCC PN6727.J573 I53 2018 | DDC 741.5/973--dc23
LC record available at https://lccn.loc.gov/2017037933

CHAPTER ONE

"BETWEEN 1889 AND 1918, 2,522 NEGROES WERE MURDERED BY LYNCH MOBS IN AMERICA. THAT WE KNOW OF.
"NOW, SINCE THE BEGINNING OF THE '30s, MOST OF THE WHITE PAPERS DON'T EVEN CONSIDER IT NEWS.
"TO THEM, ANOTHER NIGGER DEAD IS NOT A STORY.
"SO MY JOB IS TO MAKE IT ONE. THAT'S ALL."

"AFTER THEY BEAT HIM NEAR TO DEATH, THEY USUALLY CAP IT OFF WITH SOME RITUAL-- **DE-MASCULATION.**"

"DON'T YOU MEAN *'EMASCULATION?'*"

"I'VE SAID TOO MUCH, THESE HORRORS ARE OUTSIDE THE FEMALE MIND."

AAAAAAHHH!

"AFTER THAT, IT'S MEMENTO TIME. THEY TAKE PIECES OF THE BODY AS KEEPSAKES. PICTURES ARE TAKEN TO REMEMBER THE SPECIAL DAY."
GET YOUR POSTCARDS, LADIES AND GENTLEMEN! REMEMBER THE DAY THAT YOU TOOK PART IN HISTORY!
FIFTY CENTS FOR ONE, THREE FOR A DOLLAR!

"POSTCARDS? NOW ZANE, I DO BELIEVE YOU'RE HAVING A LAUGH."
"PERSONALIZED POSTCARDS, MILDRED. IT'S PART OF THE RITUAL."
ALL RIGHT, YOU HEARD THE MAN, LET'S MAKE IT ORDERLY, EVERYONE IN LINE!
I'LL PAY FOR ONE FREE PRINT FOR THE MEN RESPONSIBLE, HEROES THAT THEY ARE.

AND WE'LL NEED YOUR PERSONAL INFORMATION, FOR SHIPPING, YOU UNDERSTAND? NAME AND OCCUPATION?
SYDNEY SAUNDERS, SHOP FOREMAN AT DUNDEE'S MILL...

569 ELK HORN ROAD, PEEKSVILLE. GOT IT. AND YOUR BROTHER WAS HERE TOO?

HEY BILL, YOU CHEAP GOAT, WHEN'D YOU HIRE THIS NEW ASSISTANT? HE'S REAL ORGANIZED.
ASSISTANT? YOU KNOW I DON'T WASTE MONEY ON ASSISTANTS. I THOUGHT THAT FELLOW WAS WITH YOU.
"HOW DO YOU KEEP THEM FROM DISCOVERING YOU?"
"THAT I'M A JOURNALIST?"
"NO..."

"THAT YOU'RE REALLY A ***NEGRO.***"
"OH, THAT. I JUST DON'T STAY LONG ENOUGH FOR THOSE ***CRACKERS*** TO FIGURE IT OUT."

WELL THEN, IF YOU AIN'T USING HIM FOR MAILINGS, HOW COMES HE'S GONE AND GOT EVERYBODY'S NAMES AND ADDRESSES FOR?
"AT LEAST I TRY NOT TO GET CAUGHT. BUT SOMETIMES..."

"WHAT DO YOU DO THEN? WHAT DID YOU DO THIS TIME?"
"I DID WHAT ANY SELF-RESPECTING COLORED MAN WOULD DO IN THE SITUATION."
HOW Y'ALL DOING? LET ME SAY THIS IS A LOVELY LYNCHING YOU'RE THROWING HERE.

"I RAN."
GET HIM!

"LIKE BEIGE LIGHTNING GOING DOWNHILL. I RAN."
THAT'S A NIGGER! GET THAT NIGGER!
"SORRY TO INTERRUPT YOUR CHAT WITH MY GIRL, ZANE, BUT NOW I MUST JUMP IN: NOW YOU JUST BRAGGING."
"CARL, STOP. THEN WHAT HAPPENED? HOW DID YOU GET BACK TO HARLEM, SAFE?"

"I JUST GOT LUCKY."
"THAT I DON'T BELIEVE."
"I DO, HONEY. THE WAY I AM WITH CARDS AND THE LADIES, ZANE IS WITH LIFE."

"CARL'S RIGHT, MILDRED. I AM STUPIDLY, IMPOSSIBLY LUCKY."

"THAT'S WHY I CAN'T BE DOING THIS STUFF NO MORE."
"JOKING ASIDE, ZANE, WHAT YOU DO IS A GREAT SERVICE TO OUR PEOPLE. YOU'RE NOT JUST PASSING FOR WHITE TO GET A TABLE AT THE WALDORF-ASTORIA."
"NOW HONEY, I TAKE OFFENSE TO THAT. CAN'T A BLACK MAN EAT A WALDORF SALAD WITHOUT BEING BRANDED A RACE-TRAITOR?"

"YOU GOT TO ADMIT, SLICK, YOU GOT A SKILL FOR AVOIDING THE DEVIL."
"THAT JUST MEANS THAT NOW THE DEVIL'S OUT THERE, LOOKING FOR ME--"

--AND THAT THE DEVIL IS VERY MAD.
LADIES AND GENTLEMEN, THE FAMOUS INCOGNEGRO HIMSELF, DEATH-DEFYING UNDERCOVER OCTOROON OF THE MODERN AGE!
MY BUDDY ZANE, THE HIGH-YELLOW SUPER NEGRO! ABLE TO PASS FOR A NORDIC IN THE BLINK OF AN EYE.
New Holland Herald
LYNCHING IN TUSCALOOSA

BUT I'M NOT FAMOUS. THAT'S SORT OF THE POINT.
OF COURSE YOU'RE FAMOUS. EVERYONE READS YOUR INVESTIGATIONS INTO THE LYNCHING PROBLEM. ALL OF HARLEM KNOWS INCOGNEGRO.
EXACTLY, EVERYONE KNOWS WHO "INCOGNEGRO" IS, BUT "ZANE PINCHBACK" IS A NOBODY. IT IS THE AGE OF THE BLACK WRITER, AND ZANE PINCHBACK HAS DONE NOTHING, IT APPEARS.

THAT'S ABSURD. YOU'RE PUBLISHED IN EVERY BLACK PAPER AND PAMPHLET IN THE NORTH.
IF IT WASN'T FOR YOUR INVESTIGATIVE WORK, MANY OF THESE LYNCHINGS WOULD NEVER BE REVEALED.

BUT I WANT TO BE REVEALED TOO. THERE IS A MOVEMENT HAPPENING RIGHT HERE IN HARLEM, A RENAISSANCE. I'M A WRITER. HOW COULD I NOT WANT TO BE A PART OF THAT?
GEORGE SCHUYLER, THE COLUMNIST FROM THE MESSENGER, EVEN HE'S GOT A NOVEL COMING OUT.

ANSWER'S SIMPLE. KEEP UP THE INVESTIGATIVE STUFF YOU'RE KNOWN FOR, BUT PUBLISH UNDER YOUR OWN NAME AND PICTURE. WE COULD HAVE A BIG COMING OUT PARTY AT SMALL'S PARADISE, LADIES FREE BEFORE TEN. CASH BAR, OF COURSE.
CARL, THAT IS A THOROUGHLY BAD IDEA.
WELL, YOU COULD DO AN OPEN BAR IF THE HERALD WILL PAY FOR IT.

IF I PUBLISH UNDER MY NAME AND PICTURE, I CAN NEVER DO UNDERCOVER AGAIN.
THE PRICE OF FAME, CHAPPIE. THE PRICE OF FAME.

YOU JOKE, CARL, BUT WHAT ARE *YOU* DOING? WHAT HAVE YOU DONE? WHAT ARE YOU EVEN SERIOUS ABOUT?

I'M SERIOUS. I'M *SERIOUS* ABOUT LOOKING CUTE FOR YOU, SUGAR MAMA. I'M SERIOUS ABOUT WANTING YOU TO BE MY LAWFULLY WEDDED WIFE. AND WHAT I *HAVE* DONE IS PUT A MASSIVE ROCK ON YOUR FINGER.

AND THIS IS THE ONLY THING THAT IS BUYING YOU TIME. TILL YOU BECOME *SOMEONE* TO MARRY.

MAN, I LOVE THAT WOMAN, BUT SHE IS ONE DICTY MUSTARD-SEED.
IF SHE EVER FINDS OUT I WON THAT RING PLAYING BID WHIST BEHIND THE Y, SHE'S LEAVING ME FOR SURE.

YOU WANT TO GAIN HER *RESPECT?* GET A JOB. PLAYING CARDS FOR RENT MONEY ISN'T ENOUGH. YOU KNOW HALF OF HARLEM, I'M SURE YOU COULD SCROUNGE UP SOMETHING *RESPECTABLE.* I HEAR THE POST OFFICE EXAM IS COMING UP-- THEY HIRE NEGROES.
NEGRO, PLEASE. THE POST OFFICE.
I NEED *ADVENTURE.* I NEED TO MAKE *MY* NAME TOO, THEN I'LL BE COPACETIC.

WELL, YOU TAKE *MY* JOB THEN. BECAUSE FIRST THING TOMORROW, I'M GOING IN THERE AND TELLING HARRISON THAT I'M DONE.

LIKE HELL YOU IS.
YOU'RE GOING TO GET YOUR YALLER ASS BACK OUT THERE AND GET ME A STORY, THAT'S WHAT YOU GOING TO BE DOING.

COME ON, BOSS. YOU'VE BEEN DANGLING THAT MANAGING EDITOR JOB IN FRONT OF ME FOR YEARS. AND I'M NOT TALKING ABOUT KILLING THE COLUMN, JUST GOING LOCAL. I WANT SOME RECOGNITION FOR A CHANGE.
New Holland Herald

OH, SO YOU GOING LOCAL? NEGRO, I GOT LOCAL COLUMNISTS. I GOT MORE LAZY, NON-INVESTIGATING, PONTIFICATING BLOWHARD COLUMNISTS THAN I NEED.
BUT WHAT I ONLY HAVE ONE OF, AND WHAT NOBODY ELSE HAS, IS A WHITE NIGGER COLUMNIST MAD ENOUGH TO GO OUT AND GET THE STORY FROM HELL ITSELF.

SEE, THAT'S IT, BOSS. I'M NOT THAT MAD ENOUGH ANYMORE.
OH YEAH? HAVE A SEAT, LET ME SHOW YOU SOMETHING.

LIKE I WAS TRYING TO TELL YOU, TAKE A LOOK AT THESE WIRE CLIPPINGS THAT JUST CAME IN BEFORE YOU SAY ANYTHING ELSE.
Tupelo Mississippi-URGENT

IF THIS IS ANOTHER ATTEMPT TO KEEP ME--
LOOK AT THE NAME. LOOK AT THE DATES. I'M NOT TRYING TO SHIT YOU, ZANE. IT JUST CAME IN LAST NIGHT.

GODDAMMIT. GOD DAMN IT.

MAYBE HE DID.

ALL RIGHT, FINE, I'M ON THIS LAST STORY. BUT THIS CHANGES NOTHING. WHEN I COME BACK, I BETTER HAVE AN OFFICE. AND IT BETTER SAY MANAGING EDITOR ON THE DOOR.

MAKE IT BACK, AND MAKE IT BACK SAFE, AND I'LL GIVE YOU THAT AND A COLUMN, WITH YOUR PICTURE ON THE FRONT.
BUT NOT A RAISE.

YOU READY FOR LUNCH THEN? I WAS THINKING WE COULD DO THE ALGONQUIN, SWIM AMONGST THE PINKIES FOR A BIT.
I CAN'T. SOMETHING'S COME UP.
COME ON, WHATEVER IT IS, BLOW IT OFF. IF YOU'RE SICK OF THE OFAYS, THERE'S A NEW BAR ON LENOX WE MUST CHECK OUT.

LIFE IS NOT ALL BAR STOOLS AND RENT PARTIES, CARL. SOMETIMES A MAN HAS TO DO SOMETHING, AND RIGHT NOW I HAVE TO BE ON THE 8:13 CAROLINIAN EN ROUTE TO YAZOO CITY.

HEY, I DON'T NEED THAT FROM YOU, TOO! I'M ABOUT TO MAKE MOVES, SLICK! YOU WATCH ME!

I AM INCOGNEGRO.
I DON'T WEAR A MASK LIKE ZORRO OR A CAPE LIKE THE SHADOW, BUT I DON A DISGUISE NONETHELESS.

MY CAMOUFLAGE IS PROVIDED BY MY GENES; THE PRODUCT OF THE SOUTHERN TRADITION NOBODY LIKES TO TALK ABOUT. SLAVERY. RAPE. HYPOCRISY.
AMERICAN NEGROES ARE A MULATTO PEOPLE; I'M JUST AN EXTREME EXAMPLE. A WALKING REMINDER.

SINCE WHITE AMERICA REFUSES TO SEE ITS PAST, THEY CAN'T REALLY SEE ME TOO WELL, EITHER.

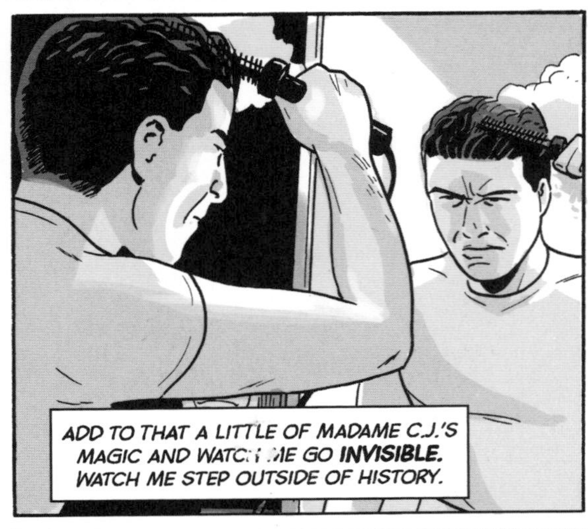
ADD TO THAT A LITTLE OF MADAME C.J.'S MAGIC AND WATCH ME GO INVISIBLE. WATCH ME STEP OUTSIDE OF HISTORY.

ASSIMILATION AS REVOLUTION.

THAT'S ONE THING THAT MOST OF **US** KNOW THAT MOST WHITE FOLKS DON'T. THAT RACE DOESN'T REALLY EXIST.
CULTURE? ETHNICITY? SURE. CLASS TOO. BUT **RACE** IS JUST A BUNCH OF **RULES** MEANT TO KEEP US ON THE BOTTOM.

RACE IS A **STRATEGY.**
THE REST IS JUST PEOPLE **ACTING.** PLAYING ROLES.

THAT'S WHAT WHITE FOLKS NEVER GET. THEY DON'T THINK THEY HAVE **ACCENTS.** THEY DON'T THINK THEY EAT **ETHNIC** FOODS. THEIR MUSIC IS **CLASSICAL.**
THEY THINK THEY'RE JUST **NORMAL.** THAT THEY ARE THE **UNIVERSAL,** AND THAT EVERYONE ELSE IS AN ODD **DEVIATION** FROM FORM.

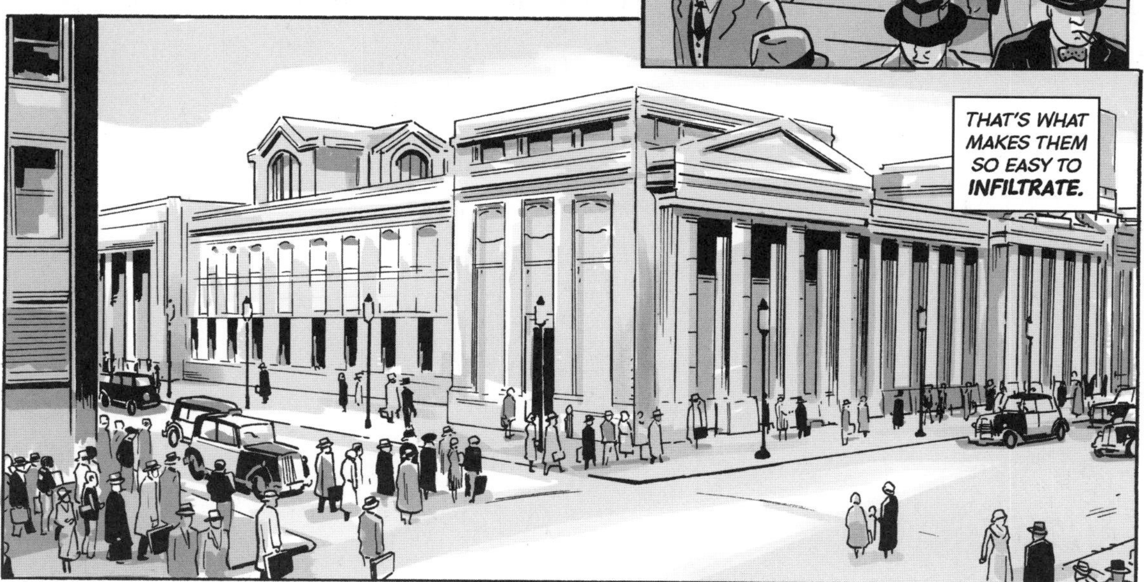
THAT'S WHAT MAKES THEM SO EASY TO **INFILTRATE.**

FIRST STOP, NEWARK, NEW JERSEY!
NEWARK, NEW JERSEY NEXT STOP!

EXCUSE ME, IS THIS SEAT AVAILABLE?
YES IT IS, BE MY GUEST.

I DO BELIEVE, IS THAT THE MIGHTY MISSISSIPPI I HEAR ROARING THROUGH YOUR VOICE? I'M FROM KOKOMO! WHERE YOU FROM?
PEEKS COUNTY, MYSELF. UP ON VACATION?

OH NO, JUST A LITTLE QUICK BUSINESS, THAT'S ALL. ME, I CAN'T STAND IT UP IN NEW YORK. IT'S A BESTIAL CITY. JUST BESTIAL.
I COULDN'T AGREE MORE.

I WAS DYING TO GET OUT OF THERE. TOO MANY NEGROES, IF YOU ASK ME.

OH, I WOULDN'T SAY THAT. BACK IN KOKOMO, WE HAVE MORE THAN OUR FAIR SHARE OF THE NIGGRAS, AND I MUST SAY YOU WOULD FIND MY CITY THE MOST PLEASANT OF LOCALES. DECENT PEOPLE, THE COLORED FOLK ARE.
YOU DON'T SAY? WELL THAT DOES WARM THE HEART.
I THINK WHAT YOU ARE REFERRING TO IS THE TYPE OF NIGGRAS THEY GOT UP HERE IN THE NORTH. THEY'RE UPPITY, DON'T KNOW THEIR PLACE.
IT'S SAD, REALLY. THE CARPET-BAGGERS DON'T LOVE THEIR NIGGRAS LIKE WE DO DOWN HOME. THEY NEGLECT THEM. THEY LET THEM GROW WILD.
IF I HAD THE TIME AND ENERGY, I'D TAKE MY CAT OF NINE RIGHT UP THERE TO HARLEM AND WHIP SOME SENSE INTO THOSE ZIP COONS FOR THEIR OWN--
MOTHERFUCKER, I WILL WHUP YOUR NATURAL BORN CRACKER ASS!
CARL! STOP! STOP!
GAAK!

WHAT THE HELL ARE YOU DOING?
LET ME GO! DID YOU HEAR THAT SON OF A BITCH?

AMERICA IS NOT 135TH STREET, CARL. YOU CAN'T JUST ATTACK WHITE MEN WHEN THEY SAY SOMETHING RACIST.
WHAT THE HELL ARE YOU EVEN DOING HERE?

I'M HERE TO MAKE MY MOVE.

YOU'RE GOING SOUTH ON ANOTHER STORY. THIS TIME I'M COMING WITH YOU. SHOW ME WHAT YOU DO, HOW YOU DO IT. THEN WHEN YOU QUIT, I CAN DO THE JOB. THEN EVERYONE'S HAPPY.
CHAPPIE, THAT IS SO STUPID, ON SO MANY LEVELS. FIRST, I'VE NEVER SEEN YOU WRITE EVEN A PARAGRAPH--
I CAN WRITE.
REGARDLESS, NOT THIS TRIP. NOT RIGHT NOW. YOU'RE GOING BACK. YOU'RE GETTING OFF IN TRENTON, AND YOU'RE GOING BACK TO HARLEM. THAT'S FINAL.

YOU DON'T GET IT, DO YOU? THAT'S THE POINT: I'M NOT A BOY WHO CAN BE ORDERED AROUND ANYMORE. IT'S MAN TIME.
I'M GOING SOUTH, AND I'M GOING TO TUPELO. SO YOU CAN SHOW ME THE ROPES OR WATCH ME GET ROPED, ONE WAY OR THE OTHER.

DO YOU HONESTLY BELIEVE, IN YOUR LITTLE MONKEY MIND, THAT WE'RE GOING TO LET YOU ONTO THAT TRAIN? EVEN IN THE COLORED SECTION?
WHY DON'T YOU JUST GET BACK TO YOUR OLD MAN AND OLD MULE AND ROLL BACK TO WHERE YOU BELONG?
WHERE'D YOU GET THE MONEY FOR THAT TICKET? YOU STEAL IT? EVERYBODY KNOW NIGGERS DON'T HAVE NO MONEY.

TUPELO, MISSISSIPPI. JUST LIKE I PICTURED IT.
DON'T LOOK. DON'T STARE. REMEMBER WHAT WE'VE BEEN TALKING ABOUT. BLEND. NOTICE. DON'T GET DIRECTLY INVOLVED.
COLORED

BULLSHIT. WHAT'S THE POINT OF BEING HERE IF WE DON'T DO *SOMETHING?*
FINE! JUST STOP. LET **ME** TRY, THEN.

WHAT'S A MATTER, BOY? YOU THINK YOU'RE TOO GOOD FOR MISSISSIPPI? YOU TRYING TO RUN OUT?

WHO THE **HELL** IS YOU?
YOU'RE TALKING TO A ***KLOREROE*** IN THE KLAN HIMSELF, JUST GOT OFF THE TRAIN. WORD IS IN BILOXI THAT YOU ALL HAVING TROUBLE TAKING CARE OF YOUR NIGGERS. *AYAK?**
*ARE YOU A KLANSMAN?

*AKIA.** STRANGER, WE DON'T NEED NO HELP FROM BILOXI. WE KNOW HOW TO HANDLE OUR NIGGERS JUST FINE.
OH YEAH? THEN WHY ARE YOU ACTUALLY TRYING TO KEEP ONE AROUND? IF THE DAMN FOOL WANTS TO LEAVE...
*A KLANSMAN I AM

GET THE HELL OUT OF HERE. GO BACK TO AFRICA, WHILE YOU'RE AT IT. DECENT FOLKS AIN'T TAKING YOUR KIND NO MORE.

GIT! AND DON'T COME BACK HERE, NIGGER! GIT NOW!

SPREAD THE WORD! THE NATIONAL OFFICE IS IN TOWN!
ZANE, YOU ARE OFFICIALLY THE CRAZIEST NIGGER SOUTH OF THE MASON-DIXON. MY PAL.

BOSS, YOU NEED A RIDE TO TOWN? I'M GOING.
SEE, THAT'S THE SOUTHERN HOSPITALITY I'D HEARD SO MUCH ABOUT.

HOW THE HELL DO THEY LIVE DOWN HERE? IF IT'S THIS BAD, WHY DON'T THEY ALL JUST GO NORTH?

LOTS OF FOLKS DO. BUT IT AIN'T ALL BAD AND IT AIN'T ALWAYS THIS BAD. THERE'S BEEN-- TROUBLE. GOT FOLKS RILED.
WHAT KIND OF TROUBLE?

A WOMAN WAS FOUND KILLED. MICHAELA MATHERS, OUT IN THE WOODS PAST TOWN. BUT THEY CAUGHT A MAN, THINK THEY GOT THE RIGHT ONE.
WHAT DO YOU THINK? YOU THINK THEY GOT THE RIGHT ONE?

DON'T MATTER WHAT I THINK. BUT THEY GOT ALONZO PINCHBACK, THAT BOY THEY CALL PINCHY, LOCKED UP DOWN THE SHERIFF'S. SUSPECT HE'LL PAY FOR IT.
PINCHBACK?

I SAW WHAT YOU DID BACK THERE. MY NAME'S RYDER; THAT WAS MY SON. LONG AS YOU'RE IN TOWN, I OWE YOU ONE.
GOOD. 'CAUSE I'M GOING TO NEED ONE.

PINCHBACK? HE SAID PINCHBACK, AM I RIGHT? WHAT THE HELL'S GOING ON HERE?
I'LL TELL YOU LATER. JUST GO AND FIND US SOMEPLACE TO STAY. SOMEPLACE QUIET, OKAY?
SOMEPLACE LOW PROFILE. ANYBODY ASKS ABOUT ME, HINT THAT I'M FROM THE KLAN; THAT SHOULD COVER US FOR NOW.

AND CARL, CUT THE SOUTHERN ACCENT; IT'S HORRENDOUS. JUST STAY OUT OF TROUBLE AND I'LL MEET YOU BACK AROUND HERE IN AN HOUR.
COME ON, Z. A LITTLE TROUBLE MAKES THE WORLD GO AROUND.

SHERIFF

I DON'T CARE WHO YOU ARE OR WHAT YOU'RE SELLING. WE GOT ENOUGH GOING ON AROUND HERE WITHOUT ANY MORE BEING BROUGHT IN.
GOOD TO MEET YOU TOO, SIR, BUT YOU BEST LISTEN TO ME OR YOU MIGHT NOT GET A CHOICE. AYAK?

SHERIFF, DEPUTY, CATCH RECORD STRIPER ON LUNCH
AY-WHAT? LOOK, I'M ALREADY SHORT MY DEPUTY, SO I DON'T HAVE TIME FOR THIS SHIT. WHAT DO YOU WANT?

I'M REPRESENTING A LARGER SOUTHERN CONCERN, A BROTHERHOOD I'M SURE YOU ARE AWARE OF. I WAS SENT FROM BILOXI TO MAKE SURE THINGS GO WELL WITH THIS PINCHBACK INCIDENT.
WHAT? LOOK, I DON'T NEED A BUNCH OF VIGILANTES FROM OUT OF TOWN POKING IN ON MY BUSINESS. I DON'T NEED YOUR HELP, I DON'T WANT IT, AND I DON'T CARE FOR IT.

SHERIFF. THAT'S AN ELECTED OFFICE 'ROUND THESE PARTS, ISN'T IT? YOU TELLING ME YOU DON'T CARE WHAT PEOPLE THINK, POWERFUL PEOPLE? THINK ABOUT THAT.

FINE. JUST CUT TO IT THEN. WHAT THE HELL DO I HAVE TO DO TO GET YOU THE HELL OUT OF MY OFFICE?

LET ME SEE THIS NIGGER, THROW A COUPLE QUICK QUESTIONS AT HIM MYSELF. THEN I CAN GO BACK AND TELL MY PEOPLE, SPREAD THE WORD THAT YOU'RE DOING A GOOD JOB, AND EVERYONE'S HAPPY.
YOU MIGHT EVEN AVOID THE MOB THAT I SEE IS BUILDING OUT THERE.

FINE. YOU GOT FIVE MINUTES. THE BOY AIN'T SAID HARDLY NOTHING FOR THE LAST WEEK, SO YOU SEE HOW YOUR LUCK'S ANY DIFFERENT.

HEY ASSHOLE, SEE WHAT'S WAITING FOR YOU? YOU GOT YOU A VISITOR FROM THE KNIGHTS OF THE KU KLUX KLAN. CAME ALL THE WAY FROM BILOXI JUST FOR YOUR CARCASS.
YOU GET A LOAD OF HIM, THEN YOU THINK ABOUT WHERE YOUR SILENCE IS GETTING YOU.

ALONZO. COME HERE, HURRY.
ALONZO! QUICKLY, HE WON'T BE GONE LONG. ALONZO!
NOBODY CALLS ME THAT.

MOM DID. DAD DID TOO WHEN HE USED TO TAKE A STICK TO YOUR BUTT.

ZANE?!

LORDY, BROTHER. YOU NOT ONLY GONE OFAY ON US, YOU JOINED THE GODDAMN KLAN.

YOU'RE A FOOL, YOU KNOW THAT? HERE YOU ARE ABOUT TO GET KILLED AND YOU STILL ACTING CRAZY.
SHIT, NOT HALF AS CRAZY AS YOU SHOWING YOUR YALLER ASS IN THIS PLACE, BRUH.

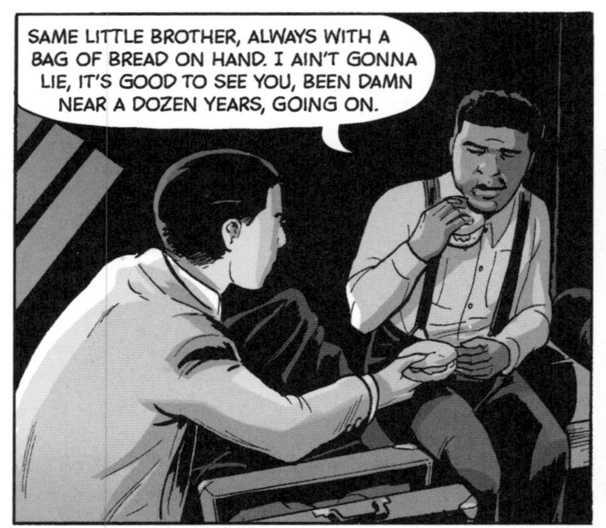
SAME LITTLE BROTHER, ALWAYS WITH A BAG OF BREAD ON HAND. I AIN'T GONNA LIE, IT'S GOOD TO SEE YOU, BEEN DAMN NEAR A DOZEN YEARS, GOING ON.

THAT SAID, YOU NEED TO TURN AROUND, GO BACK UP NORTH BEFORE THEY ***HANGING*** TWO OF MARION'S LITTLE BOYS INSTEAD OF ONE.
I'M HERE, PINCHY. SO TELL ME WHAT HAPPENED. I'M NOT LEAVING WITHOUT AT LEAST TRYING SOMETHING.

"NOTHING TO TELL. THERE I WAS ON THE HILLSIDE ABOUT FOUR MILES FROM TOWN. ***MINDING*** MY OWN, JUST WALKING THROUGH THE WOODS ON A LITTLE NATURE STROLL--"
"STOP."

LOOK, YOU LIKE NATURE ABOUT AS MUCH AS YOU LIKE TAKING A BATH. CUT THE SHIT AND TELL ME WHAT'S GOING ON SO I CAN HELP YOU.

"OKAY, FINE. SORRY. SO I BEEN SETTING UP A STILL OUT ON THAT HILLSIDE. REGULAR TENNESSEE-STYLE *MOONSHINE* LIKE UNCLE JIM TAUGHT ME. I MET THE LOVE OF MY LIFE, MICHAELA MATHERS--"
"THE DECEASED WHITE WOMAN, ALONZO?"
"THE LOVE OF MY LIFE, ZANE! MET HER IN MEMPHIS, AND SHE GOT ME UP HERE SIX MONTHS AGO TO HELP HER GET THIS STILL RUNNING FOR HER, HELP HER PAY OFF HER DEBTS."

SO I WAS SUPPOSED TO MEET HER OUT THERE, AND I WAS ALREADY GETTING WORRIED BECAUSE, YOU KNOW, THESE *PEOPLE* SHE OWED MONEY TO AREN'T THE PATIENT TYPES.
PLUS, IF THEY EVER FIND OUT ABOUT US... WELL, YOU KNOW. WASN'T FOR SIPPING THE SHINE, I WOULDN'T HAVE NO NERVES AT ALL.

"THEN I...I SEEN HER, WHAT THEY DID TO HER, MY ANGEL."
"YOU SAW THE *BODY?* ANYTHING YOU CAN REMEMBER?"

"BRUH, WHAT CAN I FORGET? SHE WAS SHREDDED. THAT'S THE ONLY WAY I CAN DESCRIBE IT. **SHREDDED.**
"FACE JUST... ***WASN'T*** ONE NO MORE. THEY LEFT HER CLOTHES, BUT THAT'S ABOUT IT. THEY'RE ANIMALS IN THIS COUNTY, ZANE.

"COULDN'T EVEN BURY HER. I MUST HAVE SAT THERE AN HOUR, I COULDN'T MOVE. THEN THE DOGS CAME, AND THE SHERIFF WITH THEM.
"THEM WOODS OUT THERE, THEY AIN'T RIGHT. WHOEVER, WHATEVER DID THIS, THEY GOT TO PAY. AIN'T NO LOVE IN THEIR HEARTS."

"DIDN'T EVEN FIGHT WHEN THEY TOOK ME, THAT'S HOW GONE I WAS. DIDN'T SEEM MUCH POINT TO IT."

THAT SHERIFF, HE DON'T EVEN CARE ABOUT HER. HE BEEN IN HERE, BUT ALL HE WANTS TO KNOW ABOUT IS HIS DEPUTY, AGAIN AND AGAIN LIKE I CARE A GODDAMN BIT ABOUT THAT.
NOW YOU HERE, ZANE, YOU GOT TO DO SOME-THING. YOU GOT TO TAKE CARE OF THIS.

WELL, I'M GOING TO FIND OUT THE TRUTH. I'M GOING TO FIND OUT WHO REALLY DID IT. ONCE WE HAVE THE TRUTH, THEY'LL HAVE TO LET YOU FREE.

THE TRUTH? NIGGER, WHAT KIND OF FOOL ARE YOU? THESE ARE CRACKERS, WHAT HAVE THEY EVER CARED FOR A BLACK MAN'S TRUTH?

FIRST, YOU GOING TO NEED TO GET SOME GUNS, SOME MUSCLE TOO IF YOU CAN FIND IT. THEN, YOU GOING TO COME IN HERE AND SHOOT ME OUT. AFTER THAT, WE GET THE MOONSHINE PACKED UP AND READY TO GO, AND WE GONE.
NO. THAT'S YOU BEING CRAZY AGAIN. I'M NOT A BANDIT, I'M A REPORTER. I CAN'T COME IN HERE LIKE JESSE JAMES. AND I SURE AS HELL AIN'T HELPING YOU WITH NO MOONSHINE.
WE HAVE TO PLAY THIS BY THE BOOKS, ACCORDING TO THE LAW. AT LEAST TRY TO.

FINE. BE THAT WAY, LITTLE BROTHER. I'LL JUST WAIT HERE, WHILE YOU DO YOUR BOY SCOUT NUMBER. THERE'S A **FORTUNE** IN SHINE UP IN THE HILLS. A FORTUNE. I MIGHT AS WELL BE **DEAD,** I LOSE THAT.

YOU TAKE YOUR CRACKER-LOOKING SELF AND YOU FIND OUT WHO KILLED MY GIRL, MY **PRECIOUS** MICHAELA. YOU PLAY IT YOUR WAY, AND WHEN THAT DOESN'T WORK OUT, COME IN BLAZING.
I'LL WRITE IT DOWN FOR YOU, TELL YOU HOW TO GET OUT TO THE STILL. THAT'S WHERE I FOUND HER. YOU'RE GOING TO NEED TO **POKE** AROUND.
CHECK MY STASH WHILE YOU'RE AT IT. THAT'S THE FAMILY FORTUNE.

YOU KNOW, THE WHOLE TIME COMING DOWN HERE, ALL THE WAY FROM HARLEM TO DOWN HERE, I TRIED TO PREPARE MYSELF. BUT I **FORGOT.**
THE MOST IMPORTANT THING, AND I FORGOT.
WHAT'S THAT?

HOW BIG A **JACKASS** YOU ARE.
I WAS SO WORRIED ABOUT YOU, IT COMPLETELY SLIPPED MY MIND.

BLIMEY, GENTLEMEN. BLIMEY! ALAS, I HAVE LOST ANOTHER HAND. YOU ARE TOO SMART FOR ME, BUT I BELIEVE I SHALL PARTAKE IN ANOTHER GAME AND ANOTHER GLASS OF YOUR SO-CALLED "SWEET TEA," AS YOU AMERICANS CALL IT.
GEN

WAIT A MOMENT, OL' CHAPS, I MUST TAKE A BREAK TO DISCUSS ARRANGEMENTS WITH MY BUSINESS PARTNER. TALLY-HO!

WHAT THE HELL IS WRONG WITH YOU? I TOLD YOU TO KEEP A LOW PROFILE, AND IN TWO HOURS YOU'RE ENTERTAINING THE WHOLE TOWN! AND WHAT'S WITH THAT FAKE BRITISH ACCENT? WHAT WERE YOU THINKING, CARL?
NOT A PROBLEM, MAN, NOT A PROBLEM.

YOU SAID NO SOUTHERN ACCENTS. SO I JUST TRIED AN ENGLISH ONE INSTEAD. THEY LOVE IT.

CARL, YOUR ENGLISH ACCENT IS EVEN WORSE THAN YOUR SOUTHERN ONE. YOU SOUND LIKE YOU'RE RIPPING OFF OF THE EDDIE CANTOR RADIO SHOW.
I KNOW, THEY LOVE THAT SHOW HERE. THEY DON'T KNOW A DAMN THING ABOUT ENGLAND. ONE OF THE OLDER FELLOWS OFFERED ME THREE MULES TO MAKE HIM A KNIGHT.

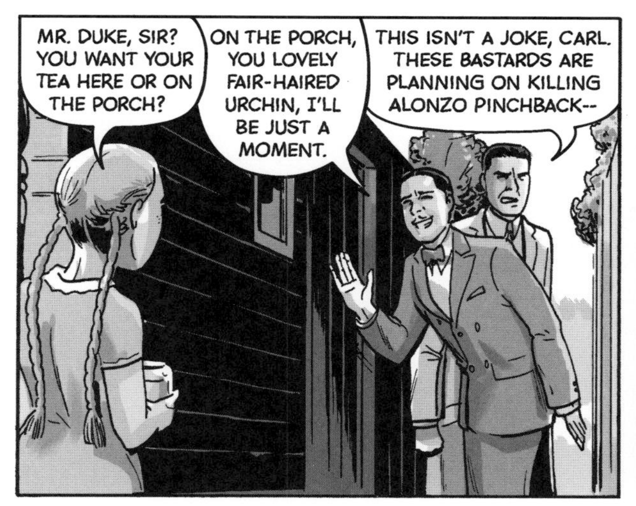
MR. DUKE, SIR? YOU WANT YOUR TEA HERE OR ON THE PORCH?
ON THE PORCH, YOU LOVELY FAIR-HAIRED URCHIN, I'LL BE JUST A MOMENT.
THIS ISN'T A JOKE, CARL. THESE BASTARDS ARE PLANNING ON KILLING ALONZO PINCHBACK--

--YOUR BROTHER.
OKAY, FINE, YOU GUESSED. YEAH, MY JACKASS OF A BROTHER. NOW I HAVE TO FIGURE OUT WHAT--
JUST BECAUSE I PLAY THE FOOL SOMETIMES DOESN'T MEAN I AM ONE.

WHAT'S GOING ON HERE IS YOUR BROTHER AND THE TOWN WHORE WERE RUNNING TAX-FREE LIQUOR IN THE NORTH HILLS. BY THE TIME SHE WAS KILLED, SHE'D SCREWED HALF THE COUNTY AND SCREWED OVER THE OTHER.
THE DEPUTY WENT MISSING RIGHT AFTER THEY FOUND HER BODY, SO MOST FIGURE HE'S THE ONE THAT KILLED HER, THEN HE WENT BACK TO HIS OWN PEOPLE IN LEWISHOM COUNTY. THEY'RE JUST GOING TO KILL YOUR BROTHER TO PUT THE WHOLE THING BEHIND THEM.

DON'T MATTER WHERE YOU GO, YOU CAN LEARN A LOT OVER AN OPEN GLASS AND A DECK OF CARDS.

OKAY, WELL... SORRY. LOOK, I'M GOING TO HAVE TO GO CHECK OUT THAT MOONSHINE STILL, YOU GOING TO BE ALL RIGHT?

ARE YOU KIDDING? I TOLD THEM I WAS IN TOWN TO BUY SOME LAND TO ADD TO MY AMERICAN HOLDINGS, AND THESE JOKERS ATE IT UP. THEY DON'T SEE A NEGRO IN FRONT OF THEM, ALL THEY SEE IS GREEN.
I MIGHT EVEN LAY ME A PINKTOES TONIGHT!

Take Bloom Street to the north of town. Walk three miles past that.

Once your feet start to **throbbing**, you'll see an old lady selling bait, that's where you want to go.

Don't talk to her, 'cause she's **touched**. Don't nobody even fish around them parts, but there she is trying to sell minnows.

Behind her shack, that's where you find the trail to my still.

Just make a left at the dead dog. Michaela done that, have mercy on her soul. To keep the kids away.

You walk about 15 minutes up that hill, you find the camp with my still.

Or probably what's **left** of my still, after the coppers have been through with it.

Salvage what you can, I'm gonna need to collect what I can before I leave town.

To go where I found the body, walk about 40 paces southeast, towards the clearing.

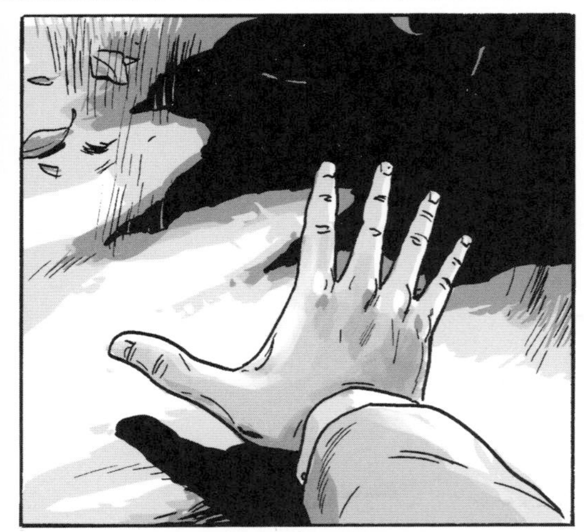

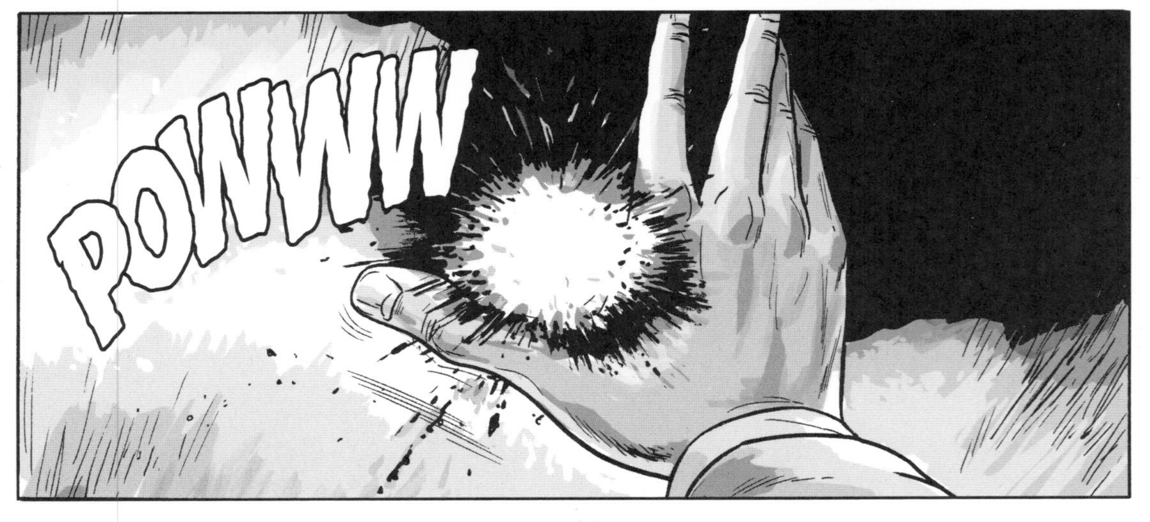
POWWW

AAAAHHH!!!!!
SHIT!

Now when you get the chance to run around a bit, I need you to go further north another 100 paces, up the hill.

WHIIIIZ!
WHIIIIIM!
This is actually the most important thing, for me being prepared to leave.

There's an old bear cave up there, and that's where I got the good stuff.

It's safe up there. I know them cops ain't never going to bother wandering uphill that far to get it.

That's the mother lode, in there. Our retirement. My biggest load, ever. How hard I worked: That's how much I loved my Michaela.

That shine. It's a masterpiece. Delicate. Love's flower.

RIIIIP
Creation itself's.

Alcohol so pure, you could drive your automobile on it.

OH LORDY JESUS, I'M ON FIRE! HELP! HELP!

AAAAAHHH!

GET IT OFF ME! GET IT OFF!

OKAY, FINE. YOU CAUGHT ME. DO WHAT YOU'RE GOING TO DO. JUST GET IT OVER WITH **QUICK.** I'M **WOMAN** ENOUGH FOR IT.
WHAT? LADY, I DON'T WANT ANYTHING TO **DO** WITH YOU. YOU SHOT MY FUCKING HAND! DO YOU SEE THIS? MY HAND!
YOU SHOULDN'T HAVE COME UP HERE TO MY STILL THEN, COMING AFTER ME. SHOULD YOU?
YOUR STILL? THIS IS SUPPOSED TO BE MY **BROTHER** ALONZO'S PLACE. WHO THE HELL ARE YOU?

WHO YOU THINK, YOU DAMN FOOL? **MICHAELA. MICHAELA MATHERS.**
WHAT A SURPRISE. PINCHY'S BROTHER, HUH? YOU SURE DON'T **LOOK** LIKE A **NIGGER.**

THERE YOU IS. I ALMOST DIDN'T COME, EVERYBODY SAID YOU WAS ALREADY IN TOWN, BUT I COME ANYWAY, AT THE TIME YOU SAID. AND YOU MIGHT ALREADY BE IN TOWN, BUT THERE YOU IS.

MR. SCHMUDT, WHAT THE HELL ARE YOU TALKING ABOUT?

SOME OF THE BOYS, THEY WENT DOWN HERE FOR THE 8:47 TRAIN THIS MORNING...
...THEY SAID SOME **BIG SHOT** CAME THROUGH **BRAGGING** TO EVERYBODY 'BOUT HOW HE WAS FROM THE NATIONAL OFFICE OF THE KLAN, BUT I KNEW YOU WERE DUE TO ARRIVE ON THE 6:13.

ANY OF YOUR FRIENDS STOP TO THINK IT WAS ODD THAT A REPRESENTATIVE OF A **SECRET** ORGANIZATION WOULD COME TO TOWN AND IMMEDIATELY START **BLABBING?**
HELL, I DIDN'T NEED TO KNOW ALL **THAT** TO KNOW HE WASN'T YOU. I JUST ASKED IF HE HAD TWO EYES.

SO, *UH*, THIS OTHER FELLA, HE ANOTHER ORGANIZER YOU WORK WITH OR SOMETHING?

I'M THE ONLY MEMBER OF THE HEAD OFFICE IN THE ASS END OF MISSISSIPPI AT THE MOMENT, LET ALONE THIS COUNTY.
SO YOU NEVER EVEN MET THIS GUY BEFORE, THEN?

OH, IF IT'S WHO I THINK IT IS, I'VE **MET** HIM.
AND I'VE BEEN LOOKING FORWARD TO SEEING **THAT** BOY AGAIN.

AAAAHHHHH!
GODDAMN IT, STOP ACTING LIKE A LITTLE PICKANINNY. HOLD STILL!

GODDAMN DEMON WATER HOOTCH!
NOW THAT'S JUST THE PAIN TALKING.

YOU JUST BEEN BAPTIZED BY THE FINEST GRADE OF MOONSHINE WHISKEY EVER SEEN IN THE STATE OF MISSISSIPPI.
AND THAT'S SAYING SOME-THING.

GOOD THING I SHOT YOU.

OH YEAH? HOW THE HELL IS THAT?

A BULLET BURNS THE WOUND, HELPS CLEAN IT SO YOU DON'T GANGRENE.
NOW IF I HAD KNIFED YOU, BE A WHOLE DIFFERENT STORY. YOU'D BE EVEN PALER THAN YOU ALREADY IS.

SO HOW THE HELL IS YOU TWO BROTHERS? YOU LOOK THE SAME IN THE FACE AND THE BUILD, AND YOU MOVE THE SAME, TALK IT TOO, BUT BESIDES THAT YOU AIN'T NOTHING ALIKE. YOU SURE YOU DON'T HAVE DIFFERENT DADDIES?
WE HAD THE SAME MOTHER. THE SAME FATHER.

HOW YOU KNOW? YOU WASN'T THERE. LOTS A NIGGERS GOT WHITE FATHERS. LOTS OF HIGH YALLER NIGGRAS GOT THEIR MASSA FOR THEIR PAPPY. MOST, I SUSPECT.
NO, PINCHY AND I ARE FULL BROTHERS. THERE'S NO QUESTION.

BUT HOW YOU KNOW FOR--
WE'RE TWINS.

DAMN. SHUT ME UP, DIDN'T YOU?

"THERE'S A YALLER GIRL OF TEXAS THAT I'M A-GONNA SEE. NO OTHER DARKIE KNOWS HER, NOT HALF AS MUCH AS ME."

NO, YOU'RE TOO KIND. REALLY, ENOUGH. ENOUGH!

SIR CARL, FORGIVE ME, BUT I HEARD THAT YOU ARE AS YET STILL IN NEED OF SUITABLE LODGING. YOU MUST THEN TAKE THE INVITATION TO STAY AT MY HOME WITH MY FAMILY AND ME.
MR. MITCHELL, OLD CHAP, MY ASSOCIATE AND I COULDN'T POSSIBLY TAKE ADVANTAGE OF YOUR AMERICAN HOSPITALITY.

NONSENSE. I HAVE AN ENTIRE GUESTHOUSE THAT'S JUST WASTING, I ASSURE YOU. AND A WIFE AND TWO DAUGHTERS WHO INSIST THEY'RE WASTING IN BOREDOM. IT WOULD BE AN HONOR.
BLIMEY, NOW I SEE WHY WE LOST TO YOU YANKS IN THE WAR OF INDEPENDENCE: YOUR GENEROUS SPIRITS! YOU ARE TOO KIND!

YOU ARE TOO KIND. BUYING DRINKS FOR A STRANGER IS ONE THING, BUT BRINGING ONE INTO YOUR HOME--
--IS A SINGULAR COUP, ONE THAT THE WHOLE OF TALLAHATCHIE COUNTY WILL SOON BE JEALOUS OF.

HOW YOU GOING TO AFFORD TO PUT UP A FANCY TYPE LIKE THIS FELLA? YOU IS A CASH-POOR MAN, AS YOU WAS JUST LAMENTING THE EVENING PAST.
EXACTLY, BUT I'M A LAND-RICH MAN. AND WORD IS HE'S BUYING UP PROPERTY BY THE DOZEN ACRE.
THE RICH FOLKS ARE RUNNING OUT OF HUNTING GROUND OVER THERE, APPARENTLY. THEY NEED FOXES, OR SOMETHING. SOME-THING LIKE THAT.

SEE THAT'S YOUR PROBLEM, YOU LOOK AT THIS MAN AND YOU SEE AN ODD, UN-AMERICAN NANCY-BOY. I LOOK AND I SEE DUCATS. I SEE MY WINDFALL.
YEAH, BUT HOW YOU KNOW THIS GUY ISN'T REALLY BROKE? OR IS EVEN WHO HE SAYS HE IS? WHAT WILL YOU DO IF HE TURNS OUT TO BE A FRAUD?

I SUSPECT I'D HAVE TO KILL HIM, THEN.
THEN FEED HIM TO MY HOGS.

"NOT MUCH OF A STORY TO TELL REALLY. I WAS JUST OUT HERE, TAKING CARE OF BUSINESS. WORKING ON THE STILL, GETTING THE BATCH READY TO GO."
COME ON, MOON! COME DOWN HERE AND FIGHT ME. I DARE YA!

"WENT TO HAVE A SMOKE. YOU KNOW, THINKING OF SAFETY, AWAY FROM THE WORKS."
GODDAMMIT, I THINKS I GOTS THE SQUIRTS.

"OVER THE MOON, I AM, OVER THE MOON"...

"THAT'S WHEN I FOUND OUT I WASN'T THE ONLY ONE OUT HERE."
KRACK

SO THAT'S IT. I FOUND A GIRL'S BODY.
WHAT DO YOU MEAN, "THAT'S IT"? YOU JUST FOUND A GIRL'S BODY? THEN WHY DOES EVERYONE THINK THAT SHE WAS YOU?

"WELL, YOU KNOW, AT FIRST I WAS PRETTY SHOOK UP. I SEEN 'EM DEAD BEFORE, BUT STILL. SHE WAS ABOUT MY AGE, MY HEIGHT. GETS YOU THINKING.
"I LOOKED AT HER AND I THOUGHT, THE WAY I'M RUNNING, THIS IS HOW I'M GONNA END UP. MORE THAN ENOUGH PEOPLE WANT TO SEE ME DEAD, JUST LIKE THIS.

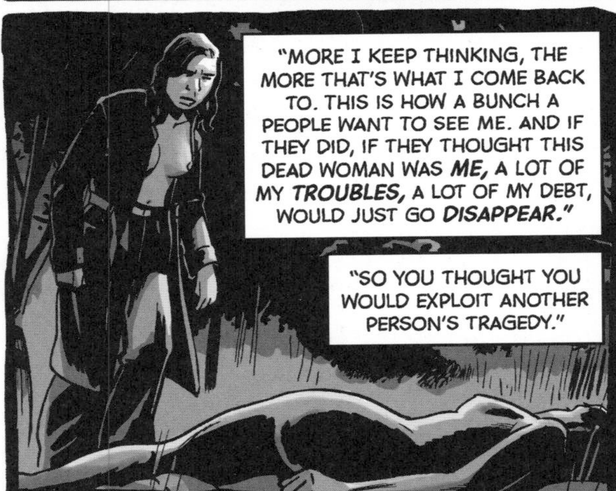
"MORE I KEEP THINKING, THE MORE THAT'S WHAT I COME BACK TO. THIS IS HOW A BUNCH A PEOPLE WANT TO SEE ME. AND IF THEY DID, IF THEY THOUGHT THIS DEAD WOMAN WAS ME, A LOT OF MY TROUBLES, A LOT OF MY DEBT, WOULD JUST GO DISAPPEAR."
"SO YOU THOUGHT YOU WOULD EXPLOIT ANOTHER PERSON'S TRAGEDY."

THERE ALREADY WAS A DEAD BODY THERE. IT SEEMED A SIN NOT TO USE IT.
SO I PUT MY CLOTHES ON HER.

"THEN I JUST GOT RID OF THOSE THINGS THAT MADE US DIFFERENT."

SO YOU DRESSED THE BODY UP. BUT HOW'D ANYONE GET UP HERE TO FIND IT?
NOW THAT I *DON'T* KNOW. I WAS GONNA DUMP IT CLOSER TO TOWN, MAKE SURE NOBODY MISSED IT.
I WENT TOWARDS THE VILLAGE TO GET PINCHY TO HELP ME, AND WHEN I CAME BACK THE BODY AND OUR STILL WAS GONE.

THIS DEPUTY WHITE, LOT OF PEOPLE THINK HE WAS MIXED UP IN THIS. DID YOU SEE HIM DUMP THE BODY OFF?
I NEVER MET THE WEIRDO BEFORE. EVEN ***I*** DON'T MESS WITH THEM ***JEFFERSON-WHITES.*** THEY AIN'T DECENT PEOPLE.

WHO ARE THE ***JEFFERSON-WHITES?***
THEY'S THE DEPUTY'S PEOPLE, WAY I HEAR IT. A BUNCH OF BACKWATER ***HILLBILLIES*** WHAT NO ONE DECENT EVEN SPEAKS OF, LET ALONE SPEAKS ***TO.***
THAT DEPUTY JUST APPEAR IN TOWN 'BOUT A YEAR PAST. THAT'S THE FIRST JEFFERSON-WHITE WHAT CAME TO SOCIETY IN ***YEARS.***

MORE I THINK ABOUT IT, YES. YES, I DID SEE SOMETHING LIKE THE DEPUTY DROP THAT POOR GIRL OFF. YUP, HE DID IT, THE ***MORE*** I THINK ABOUT IT THE MORE I'M SURE.

YOU KNOW WHAT? I BET HE DID IT AND HE RAN AWAY. I BET HE WAS SO WORRIED HE'D GET ***CAUGHT,*** HE RAN AWAY.
SOMEWHERE REAL FAR WHERE NO ONE'S GOING TO KNOW ABOUT HIM OR HIS ***CRAZY*** FAMILY. I BETCHA WE WILL ***NEVER*** SEE THAT BOY AGAIN.

HEY--
ONLY ONE THING TO DO THEN. YOU'RE GONNA MARCH INTO TOWN, INTO THE SHERIFF'S OFFICE, AND TELL HIM THAT THIS HAS ALL BEEN A MISTAKE AND YOU'RE ALIVE AND HE NEEDS TO SET PINCHY FREE.
NIGGER, HAVE YOU LOST YOUR COTTON-PICKING MIND?
THEY'RE NOT GOING TO CARE THAT I'M ALIVE, BECAUSE SOME OTHER WHITE GIRL STILL ISN'T.
THEN I'M GOING TO FIND DEPUTY WHITE, GET TO THE BOTTOM OF WHAT REALLY HAPPENED HERE.

LOOKING FOR THE DEPUTY IS A FOOL'S ERRAND, HE IS SURELY BACK IN THEM JEFFERSON-WHITE HILLS, LOST TO HISTORY.
DON'T GET ME WRONG, PINCHY IS MY SWEETHEART. BUT YOU WANT TO HELP HIM, THEN YOU GET A BIG GUN AND YOU TRY AND BLAST HIM OUT. OTHERWISE, JUST GO HOME.

YOU'RE LATE. YOU TOLD ME TO MEET YOU UP HERE AN HOUR AGO.
YUP. I'M LATE. MY *HANDS* WERE FULL.

I GOT US A PLACE TO STAY. A WHOLE HOUSE. SOUTHERN HOSPITALITY IS SOMETHING.
OH YEAH? I'VE HAD ENOUGH OF SOUTHERN HOSPITALITY FOR TODAY, THANK YOU.

DON'T THINK THAT *MATTERS* MUCH TO YOUR BROTHER...

BECAUSE I DO BELIEVE THESE PEOPLE ARE PREPARING TO *KILL* THE MAN.

I'VE GOT TO GET DOWN THERE, I'VE GOT TO GET HIM OUT OF THERE RIGHT NOW.
NOT RIGHT NOW YOU DON'T. YOU GOT ONE MORE NIGHT; THAT'S WHEN THEY'RE PLANNING IT. TOMORROW, FRIDAY, AFTER EVERYONE GETS PAID.

THEY'RE GOING TO START DRINKING, AND THEN THEY'RE GOING TO COME HERE. IT'S LIKE A FESTIVAL TO THEM.
I'VE BEEN INVITED TO A SPECIAL BANQUET BEFOREHAND, FORMAL AND EVERYTHING. THEY'RE MAKING KILLING YOUR BROTHER A HOLIDAY.

AND THEY'RE WRONG BECAUSE WE ARE NOT GOING TO LET THIS HAPPEN.

THIS DEPUTY. HE'S GOT TO KNOW SOMETHING. HE MIGHT EVEN BE BEHIND THIS. BUT HE MIGHT NOT. IT MIGHT JUST BE A RUMOR. IT MIGHT JUST BE A DEAD END.
I DON'T KNOW IF I SHOULD EVEN BOTHER TO TRY, BUT THERE'S TOO MANY PEOPLE DOWN THERE TO JUST BREAK ALONZO OUT NOW. NOT ANYMORE.

WELL, DON'T WORRY ABOUT CHOICES.
BECAUSE AT THIS POINT IT DOESN'T LOOK LIKE YOU REALLY HAVE ONE.

BANG
BANG
BANG
JOSIAH RYDER, COME OUT!

YOU TOLD ME YOU KNEW WHERE DEPUTY WHITE HAD GONE TO, DO YOU STILL THINK YOU DO?
'COURSE I DO, EVERYBODY DOES. HE WENT BACK TO SHUTTLE'S PASS. THAT'S WHERE ALL THE JEFFERSON-WHITES ARE FROM. THEY'S THE ONLY ONES WHO LIVES THERE. THEY THE ONLY ONES WHO GO THERE.

I GOT FAMILY OUT THAT WAY, I HEAR STORIES ABOUT THEM PEOPLE. THEY TOUCHED, ALL OF THEM. THE WAY THESE PEOPLE ACT, THEY AIN'T RIGHT.
THAT'S WHY NOBODY'S RUNNING TO GO LOOK FOR HIM OUT THERE. THAT'S WHY THE BOY WAS HERE FOR A YEAR AND THE SHERIFF WAS THE ONLY ONE I EVER SEEN EVEN SPEAK TO HIM.

THEN I NEED YOU TO TAKE ME THERE.
WHAT DID I DO? WHY ME?

BECAUSE YOU SAID YOU WERE IN MY DEBT, AND NOW I NEED TO CASH A DEBT IN.
BECAUSE YOU SEEM LIKE A DECENT PERSON, AND YOU CARE THAT IF SOMEBODY DOESN'T FIND THE DEPUTY, AN INNOCENT MAN IS GOING TO BE A DEAD ONE.

CORN
5¢
a
sack

I FORGOT THIS TOO.
FORGOT WHAT?

THE SOUTH. HOW BEAUTIFUL IT IS. THERE'S SO MUCH KILLING. SO MUCH STRIFE, GOING BACK, SO MUCH STRIFE.
BUT THE NATURE'S GOT NOTHING TO DO WITH THAT. THE NATURE, DON'T **NO** MAN OWN THAT. AND IT'S JUST BEAUTIFUL.

YOU FROM HERE, AIN'T YOU? NOT HERE, BUT NOT TOO FAR AWAY, AM I RIGHT?
YES YOU ARE. I USED TO BE. NOT HERE, BUT NOT FAR OFF. NOT MORE THAN A COUPLE A' DAYS, AS THE CROW FLIES. NOW I'M UP NORTH.

WHY'D YOU GO, THEN?
MY FATHER THOUGHT IT WAS BEST. MY BROTHER WAS THE PRODIGAL ONE, I WAS THE GOOD ONE. BUT IT WAS THE **OPPOSITE** OF THE BIBLE STORY.
MY FATHER FAVORED ME. HE KNEW I COULD DO SOMETHING UP THERE. MY BROTHER, HE COULD NEVER GET A BREAK. FROM MY PA OR ANYONE. SO I WENT NORTH.

YEAH, I ALWAYS HEARD IT WAS GOOD UP THERE FOR THE ***NEGRO.*** GLAD TO SEE THAT'S TRUE.

HOW DID YOU KNOW? HAVE I BECOME THAT OBVIOUS? IS MY KINK SHOWING?
DON'T WORRY. IT'S NOT LIKE THAT. I KNOW YOUR BROTHER. I AM A GODLY MAN, BUT EVEN JESUS PARTOOK OF A SIP NOW AND AGAIN.

YOU LOOK JUST LIKE THE MAN! YOU LUCKY FOLKS AROUND HERE ARE SO COLOR STRUCK OR THEY WOULD SEE IT FIRST THING TOO.

WHITE FOLKS SEE WHAT THEY WANT TO SEE. THAT'S WHAT MAKES THEM SO EASY TO FOOL WITH THIS PASSING THING.

WHITE FOLKS DO SEE WHAT THEY WANT TO SEE. AND THAT'S WHAT MAKES THEM SO DAMN DANGEROUS. IF YOU GOING TO HELP PINCHY, OR EVEN HELP YOURSELF, YOU BEST NOT FORGET THAT.

SO THIS IS SHUTTLE'S PASS. I CAN SEE WHY THE SHUTTLE *PASSED* IT.

THIS IS SHUTTLE'S PASS THE VILLAGE, NOT THE MOUNTAIN. BUT SOME OF THESE FOLK SUPPOSED TO TRADE WITH THEM JEFFERSON-WHITES. THEY COULD TELL YOU *SOMETHING,* IF ANYONE COULD.
DON'T MEAN THEY WILL, BUT THEY PROBABLY COULD. IT'S AN ODD FAMILY. PEOPLE SAY THE MEN GOT FOUR WIVES EACH. THAT SOME OF THEM IS THEIR OWN *KIN.*

PEOPLE ARE ALWAYS SAYING THOSE THINGS ABOUT MOUNTAIN FAMILIES, HALF-TRUTHS AND MYTHS. IT'S *PREJUDICE* AND WE CAN'T LET THAT GET IN OUR WAY.
A LOT IS JUST PEOPLE TALKING. BUT ALL THINGS COME FROM SOMEWHERE.
GENERAL STORE

AFTERNOON, GENTLEMEN. I'M SORRY TO INTRUDE ON YOUR LUNCH, BUT I'D LIKE A QUICK WORD.
WHO THE HELL IS YOU?

I'M FROM THE TALLAHATCHIE COUNTY DISTRICT ATTORNEY'S OFFICE AND I'M TRYING TO LOCATE DEPUTY SHERIFF FRANCIS WHITE. WE NEED *FRANCIS* TO TESTIFY IN A TRIAL THAT'S COME UP IS ALL.
PUTTING AWAY THE BAD GUYS AND WHATNOT.

SON, DON'T PAY THEM NO MIND. DID I HEAR YOU WAS ASKING ABOUT FRANCIS? FRANCIS WHITE?
WHY YES, I WAS. I WORK WITH FRANCIS BACK IN TALLAHATCHIE COUNTY.
WE'RE JUST TRYING TO LOCATE HIM FOR THIS TRIAL WE'RE PROSECUTING.

SO, UH, YOU KNOW FRANCIS? YOU A FRIEND OF FRANCIS WHITE OF THE JEFFERSON-WHITE FAMILY, YOU SAY?
SURE. HE'S A ***GREAT GUY,*** WE LOVE HIM TO DEATH 'ROUND TALLAHATCHIE WAY. ALWAYS WANTED TO SEE WHERE HIS PEOPLE WAS FROM, SO GLAD TO BE HERE.

WELL AIN'T THAT THE NICEST THING TO SAY. A ***FRIEND*** OF FRANCIS IS A FRIEND OF MINE.
LET'S GO BACK OUTSIDE SO I CAN TAKE YOU OUT TO THE COMPOUND.
MIGHTY OBLIGED.

CHAPTER TWO

OH, YOU AWAKE NOW, OKAY, BOY. TIME TO START ANSWERING QUESTIONS. WHAT YOU DONE TO OUR KIN?!

LADIES AND GENTLEMEN, IF WE COULD PAUSE FOR A MOMENT, RAISE OUR GLASSES FOR A TOAST?

FIRST, LET US ONCE AGAIN GIVE THANKS TO GOD FOR BLESSING US WITH SUCH A LOVELY MEAL. AND LET US ALSO THANK HIM FOR OUR ESTEEMED GUESTS.
AMEN!
AMEN!

AS BOTH MY WIFE AND DAUGHTER CAN ATTEST, SIR CARLTON OF LANCASHIRE IS A LOVELY HOUSEGUEST, ONE WE HOPE TO SEE MUCH OF IN THE FUTURE.

IT HAS ALSO BEEN A PRIVILEGE AND A SURPRISE TO HOST MR. HUEY, WHOM MR. SCHMUDT BRINGS TO US ALL THE WAY FROM BIRMINGHAM.
HERE ON IMPORTANT BUSINESS. DOING GOD'S WORK FOR DECENT PEOPLE.

I TOO AM HONORED, YOU KIND SIR. AND AM MOVED BY YOUR TRUST IN BRINGING A WANDERING STRANGER TO YOUR TABLE TO BREAK BREAD.

AFTER I HEARD ABOUT YOUR FOREIGN VISITOR, I TOLD MR. SCHMUDT, I JUST COULDN'T MISS THE OPPORTUNITY TO CATCH HIM.

FATHER, DON'T STEAL HIM FROM US.
SORRY HONEY, DADDY SAW HIM FIRST.

GENTLEMEN, NOW THAT THE LADIES HAVE RETREATED, LET US COMMENCE WITH THE BUSINESS OF *RELAXATION.*

YOU SIR, YOU BEEN AROUND, I HEAR. YOU STRIKE ME AS, YOU KNOW, A MAN OF THE WORLD. AM I RIGHT?

IT'S TRUE, I'VE OF COURSE BEEN AROUND EUROPE SEVERAL TIMES, HAVE A VILLA IN PARIS I'M QUITE FOND OF. AND OF LATE I'VE TOURED ASIA AND AFRICA.
WELL, I'LL BE. *WHERE* IN AFRICA?

UH... CONGO.
CONGO? ARE THEM THE ONES WHAT LET YOU SEE THEIR *TITTIES?*

YOU TALK FUNNY. DON'T YA?

I WOULDN'T SAY I TALK FUNNY, PEOPLE FROM DIFFERENT PLACES TALK IN DIFFERENT WAYS.
SO YOU SAYING *EVERYBODY* WHERE YOU FROM TALK FUNNY LIKE YOU? THAT'S CRAZY.
YOU SOUND LIKE THE BUTLER ON *THE EDDIE CANTOR RADIO SHOW.*

YUP. I'M A MAN OF THE WORLD MYSELF, TRULY. TAKE A GANDER AT THESE CARDS I WON OFF A CARPETBAGGER IN OPALIKA.

THE QUEEN OF HEARTS, SHE'S MY FAVORITE. YOU CAN EVEN SEE WHERE THE BABIES COME OUT.

YOU LIKE THEM CARDS, YOU GOT TO CHECK OUT MY OWN ***PERSONAL*** COLLECTION OF VISUAL CURIOSITIES.

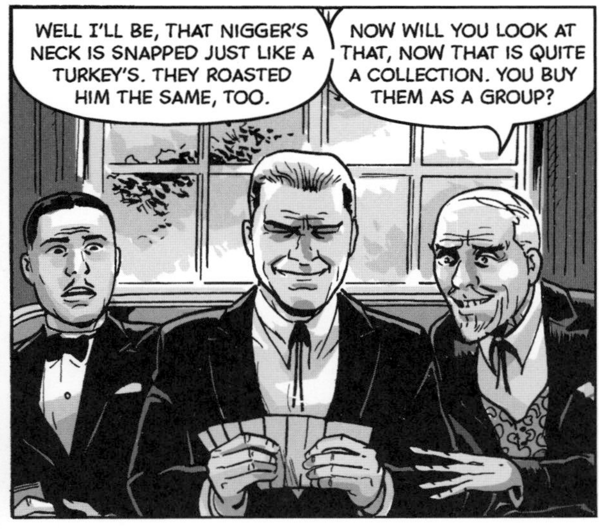
WELL I'LL BE, THAT NIGGER'S NECK IS SNAPPED JUST LIKE A TURKEY'S. THEY ROASTED HIM THE SAME, TOO.
NOW WILL YOU LOOK AT THAT, NOW THAT IS QUITE A COLLECTION. YOU BUY THEM AS A GROUP?

OH NO. I BOUGHT EACH AND EVERY ONE RIGHT THERE THE DAY THEY WERE MADE. YOU COULD STILL SMELL THE ***MEAT*** IN THE AIR.

HEY, WILL YOU LOOK AT THIS ONE, YOU GOT ONE OF A ***WHITE*** MAN GETTING THE GIBBET TOO.
OH NO, HE'S A NIGGER ALL RIGHT. HE ***LOOKED*** LIKE A WHITE MAN, BUT HE WAS JUST A NIGGER TRYING TO ***PASS.***

HOW DID YOU KNOW FOR CERTAIN?
DON'T YOU WORRY. IF THERE'S ONE THING I KNOWS IT'S NIGGERS, AND I KNOW A NIGGER WHEN I SEE ONE. NO MATTER HOW ***PALE*** HIS SKIN MIGHT BE.

BRRUUUPPPP! BLLAAAWWWKK! COUGH! COUGH! BLAAWWPP!

BLLAAAAWWK! SWEET JESUS. BLLAAAAWWK!

LORD HAVE MERCY, GIVE ME THE STRENGTH TO DEAL WITH MORE OF THIS CRACKER SHIT.

WHAT DID I HEAR YOU SAY, BOY?
WHAT'S A MATTER, YOU THROW UP YOUR ACCENT WITH YOUR SUPPER IN THERE?

I'M SORRY, KIND SIR. I DON'T BELIEVE I KNOW WHAT YOU'RE REFERRING TO.
OH, I BELIEVE YOU KNOW. AND I BELIEVE *I* KNOW EXACTLY WHO YOU ARE AS WELL.

I BEEN LOOKING FOR YOU FOR A WHILE.
TWO WEEKS BACK, IN PONTIAC, WE HAD US A LITTLE FITNESS RUN TO THE TRAIN TRACKS. REMEMBER ***NOW?***
NOW I KNOW YOU'RE CONFUSING ME FOR SOMEONE ELSE. KINDLY LET ME PASS SO THAT I MAY REJOIN MY FRIENDS.
THAT'S JUST THE THING, I MUST ***INSIST.*** WE DON'T GET A LOT OF ***CELEBRITIES*** PASSING THROUGH THE SOUTH.

AND I PROMISED MY FRIENDS THAT I WOULD INTRODUCE THEM TO THE INFAMOUS *INCOGNEGRO.*

WAKES UP!
MY OLD MAN SAY, WAKES UP! IS THE NIGGERS RISING?
COME ON, SAY SOME-THING.

I KNOW'D AS SOON AS ELMER DRAGGED YOU IN HERE. THE NIGGERS IS RISING, AIN'T THEY? JUST LIKE I BEEN SAYING, AND MY PA BEFORE ME. THE NIGGERS IS FINALLY RISING, THE DAY IS HERE.
WHAT? LOOK, THERE SEEMS TO BE SOME--
WE TOLD 'EM. WE SAID, YOU CAN ONLY BEAT A DOG FOR SO LONG. THEY GOING TO RISE UP, SLAY YOU. JUST LIKE THEY DONE THE PHARAOHS OF OLD.

LISTEN TO ME, I DON'T KNOW WHO YOU'RE TALKING ABOUT! THERE IS AN INNOCENT MAN--

SILENCE, SWEET TONGUE OF THE FOUL DEMON. YOU'RE A LIAR, I CAN SMELL IT ON YOU. YOU WALK IN LIES, YOU LIVE OFF THEM.
THERE'S A RACE WAR COMING, THAT MUCH IS CLEAR. AND THEY GOING TO WIPE OUT THE WHITE MAN WHAT KEPT THEM DOWN. MURDER THE CHILDREN LIKE NAT TURNER DONE BEFORE.

LOOK, I'M SORRY. I'M JUST LOOKING FOR FRANCIS. HE HAS TO COME BACK TO TALLAHATCHIE, IMMEDIATELY. AN INNOCENT MAN'S LIFE IS AT STAKE.

OKAY, I'MMA PLAY YOUR GAME, SPY. YOU SAID YOU KNOW FRANCIS. YOU TWO IS OLD FRIENDS, RIGHT?
HEY, I'M SORRY ABOUT THAT. I DON'T KNOW FRANCIS, BUT I KNOW A LOT ABOUT HIM, AND I THINK HE HAS INFORMATION THAT IS VITAL TO AN INVESTIGATION.

SEE, WE AIN'T SEEN OUR FRANCIS IN OVER A YEAR NOW, BUT YOU KNOW THAT. YOU'RE A SPY, AREN'T YOU, SENT BY THE NIGGERS.
PROBABLY A NIGGER YOURSELF. AS SOON AS I DROPPED MY GUARD YOU'LL TAKE ANOTHER OF MY ANGELS LIKE YOU DID FRANCIS.

THAT'S MADNESS. FRANCIS HAS BEEN WORKING AS THE SHERIFF OVER IN TALLAHATCHIE. THAT'S WHY I CAME HERE. I'M LOOKING FOR HIM TOO.

YOUR LIES REVEAL YOU, DEMON, JUST AS SURE AS THE WORD IS GOOD. FRANCIS MAY HUNT AND SPIT WITH THE BEST OF MY SONS, BUT THAT WAS JUST HER WAY.
IF YOU KNEW ANY-THING ABOUT MY FRANCIS, YOU'D KNOW SHE IS A GIRL.

SIR, LET ME HAVE HIM. I'LL GET HIM SPEAKING THE GOSPEL TRUTH.
YOU'LL HAVE YOUR TURN. THE WHOLE FAMILY WILL HAVE THEIR TURN BEFORE THE DAY IS DONE, I PROMISE YOU THAT.
HEAD OUT TO WARN THE OTHERS, MY CHILDREN. THE REVOLUTION HAS COME.

I HAVE NO KNOWLEDGE OF ANY SO-CALLED REVOLUTION, NEGRO OR OTHER.
LISTEN TO ME, THERE HAS BEEN SOME GUY OVER IN TALLAHATCHIE WHO HAS BEEN PRETENDING TO BE FRANCIS JEFFERSON-WHITE FOR OVER A YEAR.
I CAN FIND OUT IF HE HAS SOME-THING TO DO WITH YOUR DAUGHTER'S DISAPPEARANCE. YOU HAVE TO LET ME GO!

YOU'RE TRYING TO USE YOUR SILVER TONGUE AGAINST ME SO THAT I MIGHT BE VANQUISHED!

DON'T GET ME WRONG, I UNDERSTAND YOUR ANGER, CAUCA-NEGROID. THAT'S WHAT FRANCIS COULDN'T LEARN, WHAT PULLED HER ASTRAY: NIGGERS AIN'T BAD, THEY JUST BEATEN. NO POINT IN HATING THEM.

BUT LET ME GIVE SOME HIGHER THINKING TO YOU. WHAT YOU FOLK GONNA DO AFTER YOU KILL ALL THE WHITE PEOPLE? AFTER YOU TAKE YOUR RIGHTEOUS VENGEANCE?
WHO GOING TO TAKE CARE OF YOU? WHO GOING TO LEAD YOU? SHOW YOU THE WAY?

THE JEFFERSON-WHITES, THAT'S WHO.
WE'LL BE SITTING HERE ON THE MOUNTAIN, WAITING TILL YOU'RE READY. THEN I WILL SERVE AS KING OF THE NIGGERS.
YOU'RE WELCOME.

TURN AROUND AND ASK YOUR NIGGER. WE CAUGHT HIM JUST AFTER WE GOT YOU.
WE COULD HAVE KILLED THE BOY, BUT WE DIDN'T. BECAUSE I SHALL BE A JUST RULER TO THEE.

ERNEST, WATCH OVER OUR FIRST SUBJECTS AS THE YOUNGUNS FETCH THE KIN. YOU DONE GOOD, ERNEST. FOR ONCE, YOU DONE REAL GOOD, BROTHER.
THANK YOU, SEAMUS. I KNEW'D IT WAS TIME. I KNEW'D IT.

SEE, I DONE GOOD. PEOPLE TRIES TO PRETEND I'M SIMPLE, JUST 'CAUSE SEAMUS GOT THE BRAINS. BUT I DONE GOOD, SLICKER.
YOU COULDN'T FOOL ME FOR NOTHING. TAKE THAT, YOU COON-BEING SONAVABITCH!

OKAY, YOU GOT ME. I TRIED TO PULL A FAST ONE, I TRIED TO BE SLICK, AND YOU GOT ME, OKAY? JUST LET ME GO!
AIN'T GOING TO HAPPEN. I AIN'T LETTING YOU OUT SO YOU CAN WARN YOUR BRETHREN. Y'ALL DON'T KNOW WHAT'S GOOD FOR YOU.

GET OUT? I AIN'T TRYING TO GET OUT. THERE WAS SOME SENSE TO WHAT YOUR BROTHER WAS SAYING. COULD BE GOOD INSURANCE TO HAVE A MAN LIKE HIM AROUND, FOR LATER. AFTER WE KILL ALL THE OTHER WHITE FOLK.
BUT YOU GOT TO GET ME AWAY FROM THIS DARK-SKINNED NIGGER HERE, BECAUSE HE'S GOING TO KILL ME.

WHAT YOU TALKING ABOUT, YOU AN' HIM IS IN LEAGUES. I DONE SEEN YOU TOGETHER BEFORE YOU COME TO THE PUB, YOU WAS--
NO, I WAS TRYING TO GET AWAY! THAT NIGGER'S OUT TO GET ME.

DON'T YOU KNOW NOTHING?! LOOK AT ME, AS PALE AS I AM, THEN LOOK AT HIM. I'M A HOUSE NIGGER, HE'S A FIELD NIGGER. HOUSE NIGGERS AND FIELD NIGGERS CAN'T STAND EACH OTHER.
OH YEAH? SO THAT'S THE WAY IT IS, IS IT? THAT TRUE, BOY?
SURE IS. I DO BELIEVE I WANT TO KICK THIS HIGH YALLER HOUSE NIGGER'S NATURAL ASS.

WELL HELL, YOU CAN GET HIM NOW. WE GOT SOME TIME. MIGHT BE FUN, LIKE WATCHING COCKS FIGHT.

BEAT THIS FOOL GOOD, AND I'LL LET YOU GO RIGHT AWAY, HOW ABOUT THAT? YOU LIKE THAT, BOY?
YES, SIR!

YOU IN FOR IT NOW, SMARTY PANTS. SHOULDN'T HAVE TALKED TO ME THAT WAY, THEN TOLD ME THAT. I'M ONE STEP AHEAD OF YOU, ALL DAY.

NIGGERS CAN'T THINK FOR NOTHING. THAT'S WHY Y'ALL GONNA NEED THE JEFFERSON-WHITES. SOMEONE'S GOT TO DO THE THUNKING.

AH HELL.

NOT THE FACE!

HEY, PINCHY, CAN YOU HEAR ME?

WE GONNA GET YOU SOON, NIGGER. BY TOMORROW, YOU GONNA BE HANGING FROM A BRANCH LIKE A BLACK PEACH.

THEY GETTING THE BLOODLUST OUT THERE. WORSE EVERY DAY. SOON, WON'T BE ABLE TO HOLD 'EM BACK. UNDERSTAND ME?

ONLY THING HOLDING THEM DOGS AT BAY IS ME, YOU SEE? THE WAY IT IS RIGHT NOW, I'M YOUR BEST FRIEND IN THE WORLD.
I COULD BE HOME WITH MY PEG-LEGGED WIFE AND MY THREE KIDS, BUT HERE I AM, SAVING YOUR BLACK ASS.

SAVING ME FOR WHAT?

NOW SEE, THAT'S A GOOD QUESTION. SAVING YOU FOR CONVERSATIONS, I GUESS.
SEE, THAT'S OUR PROBLEM, PINCHY. WE AIN'T COMMUNICATING. THAT'S ALL I WANT FROM YOU. A WEEK I HAD YOU, AND YOU'VE SAID HARDLY NOTHING.

HOW MANY TIMES DO I HAVE TO TELL YOU, I DIDN'T KILL MICHAELA MATHERS!
EXCEPT THAT. YOU KEEP SAYING THAT.

LET'S CUT THE SHIT, THEN. I KNOW YOU DIDN'T KILL MICHAELA MATHERS, PINCHY, I NEVER THOUGHT YOU DID.

WHAT I WANT TO KNOW IS YOUR WHOLE STORY.
WHAT DID YOU REALLY SEE HAPPEN UP ON THAT MOUNTAIN?

RUFF
RUFF
RUFF
RUFF
I THINK HE'S *CLOSE.*

RUFF
RUFF
RUFF
THEY ALMOST **GOT** HIM, I'M *CERTAIN.*

HE'S *SOMEWHERE* AROUND HERE, JUST GIVE THEM A SECOND.
THEY DON'T CALL 'EM ***COON HOUNDS*** FOR *NOTHING.*

UH UH. SLOW IT DOWN, THERE. THAT'S **RUDE,** TO RUN AWAY FROM A PARTY.

WHERE'D YOU THINK YOU WAS **GOING,** MISTER FAKE ENGLISHMAN? DON'T YOU KNOW THIS IS AMERICA? AIN'T **NOWHERE** YOU CAN RUN TO THAT AIN'T THE **WHITE** MAN'S LAND.

AIN'T NO **TRAINS** OUT HERE TO DELAY MY JUSTICE **THIS** TIME, BOY.

THIS TIME, JUSTICE **WILL** BE DONE.

YOU OKAY THERE, STRANGER? NEED ANYTHING? MARTINI? SCONES?
SEE, IT'S GOOD TO FINALLY GET A CHANCE TO TALK TO YOU. WE GOT A LOT IN ***COMMON,*** I HATE TO ADMIT. SEE, WE BOTH KNOW THAT THERE'S A WAR GOING ON.
NOT CIVIL RIGHTS. ***NOT*** INTEGRATION. A ***WAR.***

WE CAUGHT US A SPY!
WE SURE DID, SCHMUDT. IN THIS WAR, HE IS A SPY. AND YOU ARE A NOBLE FOOT SOLDIER WHO I CAPTAIN.

ON ONE SIDE WE GOT GOD'S WHITE PEOPLE, AND ALL OF OUR SPOILS OF WAR. SUCH AS THIS VERY ***LAND.***

AND ON THE OTHER SIDE WE GOT ALL THE *MUD PEOPLE,* THE *INVADERS,* WHO WANT WHAT'S *OURS.*
I DON'T WANT *NOTHING* YOU GOT, OKAY? YOU FLATTER YOURSELF.
SURE YOU DO. YOU WANT OUR MONEY, OUR EDUCATION, OUR HOMES, OUR LAND. YOU EVEN WANT OUR *WOMEN,* TOO.
DON'T WASTE TIME DENYING IT. YOUR LEADERS, *WASHINGTON, DUBOIS,* THAT'S BASICALLY WHAT THEY'RE SAYING.
McFadden
GROCE
IT'S UNDERSTANDABLE. WE GOT THE BEST STUFF. WHO *WOULDN'T* WANT ALL THAT WE HAVE? BUT I'M NOT GOING TO LET YOU TAKE WHAT'S *MINE.*
I DON'T CARE IF IT'S SOME-THING I STOLE, I'D BE A FOOL IF I LET YOU HAVE IT. THAT'S JUST COMMON SENSE.
cheap
The New
and Herald
Incognegro:
LYNCHING OF FOUR INNOCENT NEGROES IN KANSAS CITY GOES UNPUNISHED
I GOT TO SAY, I'M GOING TO MISS YOUR *COLUMN,* NOW THAT YOU'VE MET YOUR RETIREMENT.
YOU SURE WAS FANCY WITH WORDS. *INCOG-NEGRO,* THAT WAS GOOD. 'CAUSE INCOG-*NIGGER* AIN'T GOT NO KIND OF *RING* TO IT.

INCOGNEGRO? YOU GOT THE WRONG GUY, TRUST ME. I CAN'T WRITE FOR NOTHING, I FAILED ENGLISH AT CHENEY. I'M NOT HIM.
AIN'T NO POINT IN LYING ON IT NOW, BOY. WHEN I SAW THIS PINCHBACK THING MAKING THE PRESS, I BET YOU MIGHT MAKE AN APPEARANCE. I BEEN TRACKING YOU FOR AWHILE.

THERE WAS ANOTHER ONE WITH HIM. AT THE TRAIN STATION, THEY SAID. MAYBE WE GOT THE WRONG ONE.

THAT TRUE, BOY? SOMETHING YOU SHOULD BE TELLING US?
'CAUSE WE GOING TO BEAT YOU ANYWAY, IT'D BE NICE TO KNOW WHAT QUESTIONS TO ASK.

IF YOU STUDIED ME, LIKE YOU SAY, YOU KNOW THAT I ONLY WORK ALONE. THAT'S HOW I AM.
YOU GOT YOUR MAN. YOU GOT ME.
I AM INCOGNEGRO.

I HATE TAKING ANOTHER MAN'S PROPERTY, BUT ADDING THE JEFFERSON-WHITE HORSE SHOULD IMPROVE OUR TIME. WE HAVE TO GET BACK. WHOEVER THIS *"FRANCIS"* GUY ***REALLY*** IS, HE'S OUR MAN. I ***BET*** YOU.

A ***HABITUAL MURDERER,*** PERHAPS, WHO TAKES ON HIS VICTIM'S ***IDENTITIES.***
MICHAELA MATHERS ***SAID*** SHE SAW HIM LURKING IN THE WOODS; HE WAS PROBABLY TRYING TO HIDE HIS ***KILL.***

MR. RYDER, ARE YOU GOING TO SPEAK TO ME AGAIN, OR IS THAT IT? DID I DO SOMETHING TO OFFEND YOU?
YOU MOST CERTAINLY DID. YOU ALMOST GOT ME KILLED. THAT OFFENDS ME VERY MUCH.
IT MIGHT NOT BOTHER YOU, BUT I TAKE EXCEPTION TO THINGS LIKE THAT.

HEY, THAT WAS MOST CERTAINLY NOT PART OF THE PLAN, AND FOR MY PART I APOLOGIZE. ONCE YOU TAKE ME BY THE PLACE THE DEPUTY WAS RENTING, I'LL NEVER BOTHER YOU AGAIN. YOU KNOW WHERE IT IS, RIGHT?
I SAID I DID. BUT WHY DO YOU THINK, AFTER ALMOST GETTING ME LYNCHED BY THEM CRAZIES, WOULD YOU THINK I WOULD?

BECAUSE I'M BEGGING YOU. THAT'S THE ONLY REASON I CAN THINK OF. BECAUSE I DON'T KNOW WHAT THE HELL IS GOING ON, BUT I GOT A FEELING THIS DEPUTY IS AT THE CENTER OF IT, AND I'M RUNNING OUT OF TIME.
AND I'M BEGGING YOU.

RUFF!
RUFF!
YIP! RUFF!
WHY COULDN'T THE DEPUTY HAVE BEEN A CAT PERSON?

I ALWAYS KEEP SOME ROLLS OF BREAD IN MY PACK. GO AROUND THE SIDE AND FEED IT TO THEM AND I'LL MAKE A BREAK FOR THE DOOR.
THE HELL I IS.
I'M GOING HOME TO MY WIFE, TO MY FARM, AND I'M GOING TO PRETEND THIS DAY NEVER HAPPENED.

ARE YOU CRAZY?
HEY DOGGIES! COME HERE, DOGGIES!
GRRRR!
RUFF!
RUFF!

BY GOLLY, THIS BOY IS OUT HIS MIND. AIN'T NO TWO WAYS ABOUT IT. TOUCHED. AIN'T NO OTHER WORD FOR IT.

CREEEAK

HOPE YOU DON'T MIND, I GAVE THEM ALL YOUR VITTLES. BUT THEY ACTING LIKE PUPS NOW.
I'M GLAD YOU CAME IN. BECAUSE YOU WOULDN'T HAVE BELIEVED ME.

I WAS WRONG, THE DEPUTY DIDN'T KILL FRANCIS JEFFERSON-WHITE. THE DEPUTY WAS THE REAL FRANCIS JEFFERSON-WHITE.
SHE WAS PASSING AS A MAN. WE'RE GETTING CLOSER.

NOW WHAT WOULD MAKE YOU BELIEVE SUCH NONSENSE?
LOOK AT THE SINK. A BRUSH FOR TEETH, BUT NO RAZOR? WHAT KIND OF MAN DOESN'T EVEN OWN A RAZOR?

AND THERE'S THREE SHIRTS IN THAT CLOSET, ALL THE SAME SIZE AS THE WHITE DRESS HANGING IN THERE TOO.
THAT DRESS, IT'S JUST LIKE THOSE HILLBILLY WOMEN. PROBABLY THE ONE SHE LEFT THE MOUNTAIN WITH.

YOU GOT IT ALL WRONG. I SEEN THIS DEPUTY, HE WOULD HAVE MADE ONE MEAN, HOMELY-LOOKING WOMAN.
LOOK AT THESE.

YOU'RE RIGHT, THAT IS ONE MEAN, HOMELY-LOOKING WOMAN. DETERMINED-LOOKING TOO.

DON'T MAKE NO SENSE. WHY WOULD A WOMAN DO SOMETHING CRAZY LIKE THAT?

RIGHT. NO SENSE.
WHO WOULD PRETEND TO BE A WHITE MAN IN THIS WORLD?
WHAT COULD BE THE POSSIBLE ADVANTAGE OF THAT?

SO HOW'S THIS GONNA HELP YOUR BROTHER, THEN? YOU STILL HAVEN'T FOUND THE WOMAN.
SOMEBODY ALREADY DID. SHE'S DEAD. LYING WITH A TOE-TAG THAT SAYS "MICHAELA MATHERS" ON IT.

BOOM

GODDAMN! WHY ARE PEOPLE ALWAYS SHOOTING AT ME IN THIS TOWN?!
IT'S NOT THE TOWN. IT'S YOU.
BOOM

COME ON OUT. AIN'T NO USE, I DONE SAW YOU IN THERE.
IS THERE A BACK WAY OUT OF HERE?
YELLOW MAN, DO I LOOK LIKE I BEEN HERE BEFORE?

THE WHOLE NEIGHBORHOOD MIGHT BE OUT LYNCHING IN THE CENTER OF TOWN, BUT THAT DON'T MEAN WE AIN'T WATCHING FOR LOOTERS OUT HERE TONIGHT.
MY HUSBAND WILL ARREST ANYONE THINKING DIFFERENT.

MA'AM, THERE'S BEEN AN UNDERSTANDABLE MISTAKE. I CAME BY HERE LOOKING FOR MY FRIEND FRANCIS--
DEPUTY FRANCIS DIDN'T HAVE NO FRIENDS, 'CEPT MY HUSBAND. SO YOU CAN SAVE IT TILL THE SHERIFF GETS HERE HIMSELF.

REALLY, MA'AM, THERE'S NO REASON TO BE **ALARMED.** I KNOW FRANCIS FROM BACK ON SHUTTLE'S PASS. MATTER OF FACT, I WAS JUST SPEAKING TO HIS FATHER THIS AFTERNOON. TOLD ME--
STAY BACK! STAY **BACK,** HEAR? OR I WILL SHOOT YOU **DEAD. STOP!**

CRACK

WHAMM!

I AM SO SORRY, LADY. **SO** SORRY. BUT THAT'S MY **BROTHER** THEY'RE TRYING TO KILL TONIGHT.

HOW... HOW COULD YOU DO THAT?
I DON'T KNOW. I'VE NEVER HIT A WOMAN BEFORE. I'M NOT THAT TYPE OF PERSON, IT'S JUST, THERE'S NO TIME.

WHAT? NO. HOW COULD YOU APPROACH A PERSON WITH A LOADED SHOTGUN LIKE THAT? POINTED AT YOU...!

SHE MIGHT BE BIG, BUT SHE'S STILL A WOMAN. I KNEW THAT IF I STOOD MY GROUND, STARED HER IN THE EYES, SHE COULDN'T BE COLD ENOUGH TO PULL THE TRIGGER.

I TAKES IT YOU AIN'T NEVER BEEN MARRIED?

SNEAKY HIGH-YELLOW BASTARD. WE BROUGHT HIM INTO OUR *HOME.*

NIGGER! LYING **NIGGER!**

HEY MR. COON!
NO, HONEY, DON'T THROW THAT.

WE CAN STILL EAT THAT ONE. THROW THIS ONE, IT'S ROT.

GET UP, BOY. GET UP. THE PARTY'S ABOUT TO BEGIN.

CAN'T YOU SEE *YOU'RE* THE *GUEST OF HONOR?*

CHAPTER THREE

THERE IT IS. **AMERICA.** YOU CAN SEE IT RIGHT OUT OUR WINDOW.
CHURCH-ATTENDING, MORAL-LIVING, **AVERAGE** MEN AND WOMEN IN ALL THEIR GLORY.

NORMAL PEOPLE, THEY NEED SOMETHING TO **HATE.** SOMETHING TO BLAME FOR WHY THINGS AIN'T **PERFECT** IN THE WORLD. SOMETHING TO EXPLAIN THEIR **FEAR.**

YOU WANT TO BE THAT THING **NEXT,** QUIET MAN?
THEY'RE HAVING THEIR FUN WITH SOME HOTSHOT **YALLER REPORTER,** CRAZY FOOL PRETENDING HE WAS SOME KINDA **ROYALTY.**
BUT NEXT THEY'RE GOING TO COME FOR **YOU,** AND THERE'S TOO MANY NOW FOR ME TO STOP.

YALLER REPORTER?

HERE, LET ME HELP YOU WITH YOUR *COLLAR.*
BE *CAREFUL* NOW. YOU GOT TO KEEP YOUR *BALANCE.*
DON'T WANT TO SLIP TOO *SOON* AND RUIN YOUR *GRAND FINALE.*

THIS AS FAST AS THIS THING GOES?
UNLESS YOU WANT US TO TURN OVER, IT IS.

YOU'RE TAKING US UP ONTO THAT LEDGE! THERE'S NO TIME FOR THAT, YOU GOT TO TAKE ME RIGHT INTO TOWN!
I'M TAKING YOU AS CLOSE AS MY BROWN-SKINNED SELF CAN MANAGE, WITHOUT GETTING STRUNG UP ALSO.
YOU CAN WALK DOWN FROM THERE, IF YOU THINK YOU GOT TO.

AND IT DON'T LOOK LIKE YOU GOT TO.

INCOG NIGGER
NOOO!!!

MMPH!
CONTROL YOURSELF, MAN. YOU ABOUT TO JOIN HIM UP IN THAT TREE, SO JUST CALM YOURSELF DOWN.

THAT'S CARL. THAT'S MY FRIEND. THAT'S MY BEST FRIEND. THEY KILLED HIM.
WHAT'S AN "INCOGNIGGER"?

THEY THOUGHT IT WAS ME. THEY THOUGHT HE WAS ME. THEY THOUGHT THEY HAD INCOGNEGRO.

I KILLED HIM. I GOT HIM KILLED. MY ACTIONS, MY WORK. THAT'S WHAT KILLED HIM.

PULL YOURSELF TOGETHER. LOOK AT THAT SCENE. LOOK AT WHAT THOSE CRACKERS DID. LOOK AT THEM LAUGHING.
YOU KILLED HIM? COULD YOU EVEN BE CAPABLE OF ACTING LIKE THAT?

LET'S GET OUT OF HERE. YOU CAN TAKE THE NEXT TRAIN. ENOUGH BLOOD DONE POURED. IT'S OVER.
NO.

NO. EVERYBODY IN TOWN IS OUT HERE. THAT MEANS THE JAIL ISN'T BEING WATCHED. THIS IS MY CHANCE.
I CAME FOR MY BROTHER. I'M GETTING MY BROTHER. THEN I'M GOING HOME.

SUIT YOURSELF THEN. I DONE MY BIT. YOU WANT TO KEEP ACTING A FOOL, YOU ON YOUR OWN.
WOULDN'T ASK OTHERWISE. I CAN FIGURE IT OUT. BUT JUST ONE MORE QUESTION.

HOW MUCH YOU WANT FOR ONE OF THEM BROKEN-DOWN HORSES?

SHERIFF

SLAM

LET MY BROTHER OUT.

YOU AGAIN? LET ME GUESS, GOT YOUR BLOOD UP FROM THAT BOY YOU JUST DONE MURDERED. THAT IT?
SEEMS TO BE YOU'RE CONFUSED. THE ONLY PRISONER I'M HOLDING IS A...

WELL I'LL BE.
YOU LOOK JUST LIKE HIM, DON'T YA. AIN'T THAT SOME SHIT.
YES IT IS. MY BROTHER. FREE HIM.

I GUESS AFTER ALL THIS IS DONE, THEY'RE GOING TO SAY I SHOULD HAVE LET THEM LYNCH HIM WHEN I HAD THE CHANCE.

BUT YOU KNOW YOU SHOULDN'T. BECAUSE YOU KNOW PINCHY'S NOT A MURDERER.
OH I DO, DO I? IS THAT WHAT YOU THINK?

WHAT I THINK IS THAT YOU AND DEPUTY FRANCIS JEFFERSON-WHITE WERE A LOT CLOSER THAN ANYBODY ELSE WOULD EVER GUESS.
ZANE? IS THAT YOU?

YOU'RE ALIVE! I KNEW IT! I KNEW YOU WERE TOO SMART FOR THESE CRACKERS.
YOU DON'T KNOW A GODDAMN THING.

YOU GET 'EM? YOU GOT THOSE BASTARDS THAT KILLED MY MICHAELA? *TELL* ME.
'COURSE HE DIDN'T.

AND SHE AIN'T EVEN *DEAD.*

WHAT? MY MICHAELA?
SHE'S ALIVE. *TRUST* ME, SHE SHOT A HOLE THROUGH MY DAMN *HAND* JUST YESTERDAY.
BUT HOW? *WHY?*

THOSE ARE GOOD QUESTIONS. BUT LET'S START WITH *SIMPLER* ONES.
HOW DOES THE *SHERIFF* HERE *KNOW* THAT?

YOU TWO, YOU'RE JUST LIKE EVERYBODY ELSE IN THIS BLOOD-SOAKED TOWN. YOU'RE HYPOCRITES.

HYPOCRITES?! YOU ARRESTED MY BROTHER FOR A CRIME YOU KNOW HE HAD NOTHING TO DO WITH, DRAGGING ME FROM THE SANITY OF NEW YORK TO GET SHOT AT IN THIS SHIT HOLE. YOUR ACTIONS RESULTED IN THE DEATH OF MY BEST FRIEND.
IF YOU WANT ME TO SHOOT YOU, JUST ASK. BUT DON'T INSULT ME.

THAT'S RICH. SO TELL ME, HOW DO I KNOW YOUR SCUMBAG BROTHER HAD NOTHING TO DO WITH THE MURDER?

BECAUSE YOU'RE THE ONE THAT KILLED HER.

YOU'RE LOONY. YOU DON'T KNOW WHAT YOU'RE TALKING ABOUT.
I KNOW THE BODY WAS FRANCIS JEFFERSON-WHITE.
THAT'S WHO YOU KILLED.
SHUT UP! SHUT YOUR TRAP!
I WENT OUT TO THE MOUNTAIN, MET HER WHOLE CRAZY FAMILY. I KNOW FRANCIS WAS REALLY A WOMAN. PRETENDING TO BE A MAN SO SHE COULD LIVE WITHOUT LIMITATIONS, I ASSUME. SO SHE COULD HAVE HER JOB.
AND THAT'S WHY YOU KILLED HER. YOU FOUND OUT THE TRUTH, AND YOU KILLED HER.
I DIDN'T...I LOVED THAT WOMAN!
BOO-HOO, BOO-HOO.
BOO-HOO, BOO-HOO.
YOUR DEPUTY WASN'T A MAN, AND IT SEEMS YOU AIN'T HALF OF ONE EITHER.

YOU WERE SUPPOSED TO WAIT BY THE HORSE, KEEP A LOOKOUT. THIS ISN'T A PLACE FOR YOU.
MICHAELA? BABY? THAT YOU?
YOU!

SHUT IT! I WILL SHOOT YOU, DON'T THINK DIFFERENT.
BABY, WHAT THE HELL YOU DOING ALIVE? WHERE WERE YOU?

WOMAN, DID YOU SET ME UP? YOU GOT ME IN HERE WORRYING AND YOU OUT THERE TRYING TO TAKE MY LIQUOR. AIN'T YOU!
I'M HERE NOW, AIN'T I? I DONE COME FOR YOU, IN THE END. THAT'S WHAT MATTERS.

MORE LIKE YOU HAVE NO CHOICE, NO WAY TO HAUL THE STASH WHEN EVERYBODY'S SUPPOSED TO THINK YOU'RE DEAD.

YOU KNOW, DON'T YOU? YOU KNOW WHAT HAPPENED TO MY FRANCIS. YOU KNOW WHO KILLED HER.

'COURSE I DO. I SHOT HER. NOW YOU GOT YOUR CONFESSION. YOU HAPPY?

WHY?

SHE COME UP THERE, SNEAKING UP ON A WOMAN ALONE IN THE WOODS, I THOUGHT IT WAS SOMEONE TRYING TO STEAL MY MOONSHINE, OR WORSE.

IF YOUR MAN-GIRL WANTED TO BE TREATED LIKE SHE WAS COMING FOR A TEA PARTY, SHE SHOULD HAVE WORN A DRESS.

DIE!

WHACK!

GET OFF! GET OFF OF HER! NO MAN HITS HER BUT ME!

GET YOUR GODDAMN HANDS--

NO!
VRAAMM

MI... MICHAELA? ANGEL?

I'M SORRY FOR YOUR LOSS, BELIEVE IT OR NOT. I KNOWS THE FEELING. BUT THAT **WEREN'T** NO **ANGEL.**
'LEAST NOT THE KIND THAT COMES FROM **ABOVE.**

DON'T! DON'T YOU--
SHE WAS GOING TO LET YOU ROT, GOING TO LET YOU HANG FOR HER CRIMES. YOU THINK ON THAT.

SO...ARE YOU GOING TO SHOOT US NEXT?
HADN'T PLANNED ON IT. BUT I GUESS THAT'S UP TO YOU.

I GOT MY MURDERER, DELIVERED MY JUSTICE. FRANCIS HAS BEEN AVENGED. NOBODY REALLY KNEW HER BUT ME, NOBODY KNEW HER SECRET. SHE SHOULD BE ABLE TO TAKE IT WITH HER.

THIS TOWN'S SEEN ENOUGH BLOODLETTING OF LATE. I THINK YOU BOYS SHOULD HEAD ON OUT, GIVE IT A CHANCE TO DRY.

THAT WORKS FOR ME. JUST TWO THINGS I'M GOING TO NEED BEFORE I GO. THAT IS MY MAN OUT THERE, THE ONE THOSE GHOULS MURDERED.
I WANT A LIST OF THE MAIN PEOPLE INVOLVED, FOR PUBLICATION, SENT TO MY OFFICE IN HARLEM BEFORE THE END OF THE WEEK.
AND I WANT MY FRIEND'S BODY RIGHT NOW, TO TAKE BACK WITH US.

BOY, DON'T YOU KNOW A GIFT HORSE WHEN YOU SEE IT? I'M DOING THE DECENT, HONORABLE, DOWNRIGHT GENEROUS THING BY LETTING YOU AND YOUR BOOTLEGGING BROTHER OUT OF HERE ALIVE.
IF EVER THERE WAS A TIME NOT TO ACT LIKE A DUMB NIGGER, THIS IS IT.

I MAY BE A DUMB NIGGER, BUT I'M NOT A LAZY ONE. I ALREADY WROTE AND FILED MY STORY WITH MY PAPER TWO HOURS AGO.
IT'S A SORDID TALE, ABOUT A CROSS-DRESSING CRACKER DEPUTY, AND THE ADULTEROUS SHERIFF WHO DISCOVERED HER.

NOW, IT HAS THE SHERIFF KILLING HER, AND THAT PART WILL NEED TO BE FIXED, BUT STILL, IF I DON'T SHOW UP IN HARLEM IN THE NEXT WEEK, MY EDITORS WILL RUN IT.

I'M SYNDICATED, DID I MENTION THAT? ON THE BIG STORIES, I'M EVEN IN THE WHITE PAPERS TOO.
WIRE SERVICE. MARVELS OF MODERN MEDIA.
OH YEAH, IF YOU COULD GET PICTURES OF ANYONE WHO WAS INVOLVED, THAT WOULD BE GREAT.

INCOG NIGGER

INCOG NIGGER

SO THIS IS IT. THIS IS HARLEM. IS IT LIKE YOU THOUGHT IT WOULD BE?
YUP. IT'S JUST LIKE I 'MAGINED. JUST AS BIG, JUST AS LOUD, JUST ABOUT THE SAME. I JUST NEVER IMAGINED ME IN A PLACE LIKE THIS.
WHAT THE HELL AM I GOING TO DO HERE?

WHAT CAN YOU DO? YOU CAN DO ANYTHING, PINCHY.
THIS IS THE LAND OF BLACK LAWYERS, BLACK DOCTORS, BLACK BUSINESSMEN. YOU CAN DO WHATEVER YOU WANT HERE. IT AIN'T LIKE THE SOUTH.

CAN I BREW MY MOONSHINE IN THEM WOODS THERE?
NO, PINCHY. THAT'S CENTRAL PARK.

I KNOW. THAT WAS A JOKE. BUT ME BEING HERE ISN'T.
YOU'RE RIGHT, IT'S NOT THE SOUTH. THIS ISN'T A PLACE, IT'S JUST A BUNCH OF STRANGERS PILING ON TOP OF EACH OTHER.

WE FROM THE SAME PLACE, THE SAME WOMB EVEN. IF I CAN ADJUST, SO CAN YOU. IT'S NOT THAT DIFFERENT. A LOT OF PEOPLE, BUT STILL THE SAME.
HERE, A BLOCK'S GOT ENOUGH PEOPLE FOR A WHOLE TOWN, AND IT ACTS LIKE THE SAME TOO.
YOU SHOP AT THE SAME CORNER STORE FOR A WHILE, YOU START TO SEE THE SAME FOLKS. YOU LEARN THEIR STORIES, THEIR NAMES. THEN IT DOESN'T FEEL SO BIG ANYMORE.

OKAY, FINE. IT'S JUST LIKE A SMALL TOWN. WHATEVER. BUT WHERE THE HELL DO I FIT IN? THIS PLACE AIN'T FOR THE LIKES OF ME. DON'T PRETEND DIFFERENT.
NO, YOU'RE RIGHT, THIS ISN'T A PLACE FOR A "BOOTLEGGING SCUMBAG."

BUT THIS IS NEW YORK. THIS IS HARLEM. THIS IS THE AGE OF THE NEW NEGRO.
HERE, THE POOR BECOME RICH; THE DESPISED, THE ADMIRED. YOU CAN CREATE ANY IDENTITY THAT YOU WANT.

SO THAT'S IT, I CAN JUST DECIDE TO BE A WHOLE NEW NEGRO? SO WHAT NEGRO YOU GOING TO BE, THEN?
THAT'S THE BEST THING: IDENTITY IS OPEN-ENDED. WHY HAVE JUST ONE?

SO, I BET NOW YOU ACTUALLY WANT ME TO GIVE YOU THAT OFFICE I PROMISED YOU?
HELL YES I DO.
AND I WANT THIS OFFICE NEXT TO YOURS TOO. SO I CAN YELL AT YOU THROUGH THE WALLS WHEN THE OCCASION ARISES.
GREAT. NOW I'M LOSING THE INCOGNEGRO COLUMN AND THE NEIGHBORHOOD'S GOING TO SHIT, ALL IN THE SAME DAY.
WRONG ON BOTH COUNTS. FIRST OF ALL, I WON'T BE HERE EVERY DAY.

NO. I WANT TO KEEP GOING INCOGNEGRO. SOMEBODY HAS TO. I CAN. SO I WILL.
BUT I WASN'T KIDDING ABOUT MY ARTS COLUMN. I'M DOING THAT TOO, AND I'M DOING IT IN MY OWN NAME.
I'LL JUST WEAR TWO HATS, SO TO SPEAK.

FINE. WEARING TWO HATS SUITS YOU.

YOU GET THAT PICTURE INTO THE INCOGNEGRO PIECE? NOT THE ONE THEY DID OF CARL, THE SIDEBAR REVEALING THE INCOGNEGRO IDENTITY?
YEAH I GOT IT. DIDN'T MAKE NO SENSE, BUT I GOT IT. AND IT'S IN THERE, GETTING PRINTED AS WE SPEAK.

YOU SURE THIS IS THE PICTURE YOU WANT TO USE? THIS IS YOUR CHANCE, YOU KNOW, TO GET RECOGNIZED.

THIS IS THE PICTURE I WANT TO USE FOR INCOGNEGRO. TRUST ME. IS THIS GOING TO GET PICKED UP FOR SYNDICATION?

OH SURE, ALREADY HAD MULTIPLE REQUESTS. THE UNVEILING OF THE INCOGNEGRO, THAT'S A BIG DEAL.
THIS FACE'LL BE IN PAPERS ACROSS THE COUNTRY BY THE END OF THE WEEK.
UGLY-ASS FACE THAT IT IS.

Welcome to... FAYETTEVILLE, MISSOURI
"GATEWAY TO THE WORLD"
WE GOT THAT INCOGNIGGER **GOOD** BACK IN MISSISSIPPI. YOU WON'T BE SEEING **HIM** NO MORE. GET IT? GET IT?
Saloon Bar
WE SURE **DO,** HUEY. YOU SURE GOT HIM GOOD.

AND I'M GOING TO TAKE CARE OF **YOUR** NIGGER PROBLEM, **TOO.** THAT'S HOW I **DO** THINGS.

HOWDY!

AFTERNOON. GENTLEMEN?

HOW Y'ALL **DOING?**

YOU THE ONE FROM TODAY'S PAPER, **AIN'T** YOU? THE FELLOW FROM THE **LYNCHINGS,** RIGHT?

MAYBE SO, MAYBE SO. **GIVE** ME THAT!
CCA

HEY! THAT COSTS A **NICKEL!** YOU OWE ME A NICKEL, **NIGGER!**

Sun-Herald
Today's Weather
INCOGNEGRO:
NEGRO RACE SPY'S
IDENTITY REVEALED!

HI, Y'ALL. UH, THERE SEEMS TO BE A CASE OF *MISTAKEN IDENTITY.*
THE END

Afterword

When I first wrote *Incognegro* roughly a decade ago,

I admit to thinking of it primarily as a story of the legacy of America's past. An historic tale of America's racial journey towards the present. A story about an era that directly impacts our contemporary moment, without being of the now. In 2007, as in 2017, the Ku Klux Klan had been largely diminished since its heyday, and other forms of organized white supremacy, foreign and domestic, had been repeatedly been defeated. We fought a worldwide war about this in the middle of the 20th century; you probably heard about it. I didn't write this thinking racism itself had ever left American society, or that the crippling effects of racism and prejudice in America have been arranged, but I did think that the age of organized, public, avowed mainstream white nationalism was over.

But I was naive. Writing this after the white nationalist display at the "Unite the Right" rally in Charlottesville, Virginia in August of 2017, a white nationalist protest that left one counter-protester dead in the streets, the racial dynamic of the early 20th century seems to be, in some ways, repeating itself. In the response to the gains by racial minorities, exemplified by the two-term election of the first black President, white racial resentment has reentered the American discourse as an overt, unapologetic force. Sadly, the era of racial terrorism covered in ***Incognegro*** is suddenly relevant again. So here we are again.

When ***Incognegro*** was first published, the response was beyond my expectations. It was among the first graphic novels to receive of "Books of the Times" daily review in *The New York Times*, was widely and generously reviewed across the country, and became a selected text in high schools and colleges as well. While the subject matter of American racial justice was common-place in prose fiction, it was still new territory in graphic storytelling. One of the things I was struck by in reviews was how many of the comic book critics were apparently being exposed to this major moment in history, the era of lynching, for the first time.

I, myself, don't remember a moment I wasn't aware of lynching, or the larger, constant threat of anti-black racial violence in America. My own black great-great-grandfather ran from a would-be lynching in South Carolina during the era covered in this work. I grew up with stories of him sitting in the living room of his new apartment in Chicago, years later but still with a shotgun resting on his lap as he stared at the door, waiting. But we all have different mythologies of America and its history. I am just honored to be able to expose more people to this era, and hope for some this storyline may serve as an entry point into a larger historical exploration.

Most people know the George Santayana quote, *"Those who cannot remember the past are condemned to repeat it."* Fewer people know the Kurt Vonnegut Jr. response, *"I've got news for Mr. Santayana: we're doomed to repeat the past no matter what. That's what it is to be alive."*

With both those notions in mind, here is an exploration of the past, fictional as it may be.
A tale of race and identity and terror in America.

— Mat Johnson

Warren's Sketchbook

zane
1
zane
2
Tache?
Pinchy
1

Preacher
Seamus
Zane 3 Straightened hair
Zane 4
Tache?

Harrison
Francis
(Take 2)
Michaela
2

Huey 2
Huey 3
Michaela

Reading Group Guide/Questions & Topics for Discussion

Incognegro is partially inspired by the true story of Walter Francis White, the leader of the NAACP who went undercover and even almost joined the KKK.

Why is it important for journalists of color to report on racist organizations? Why is it dangerous for them to do so?

Lynching were commonplace amongst African-American men accused of crimes in the pre-Civil Rights South..

Why do you think this was the case?
How did the "Jim Crow" laws contribute to these actions?

Zane tells Alonzo that he will be released once they find the true murderer. Alonzo and Michaela both assert that breaking Alonzo out of jail is the only way to save his life.

Why do you think they had such different opinions?

Zane and Carl are both able to pass as white, and at the end of the story the mob believes Mr. Huey to be black.

If it's impossible to distinguish race by sight, why is it so important in American society?

As Zane goes undercover, he says, "Race is just a bunch of rules meant to keep us on the bottom."

What are the rules? Are you aware of them in your daily life?

Zane says that his light skin is the genetic result of "the southern tradition that nobody likes to talk about. Slavery, rape, hypocrisy."

What do you think his family tree looks like?

Alonzo and Michaela both try to hide their interracial relationship.

Why? What consequences could each of them face if it was discovered?

In the opening scene, Zane tells Mildred that the horrors of lynching are "outside the female mind." Later, he says, "I knew that if I stood my ground, stared her in the eyes, she couldn't be cold enough to pull the trigger," even though he was recently shot by a woman.

What does this tell you about Zane's opinion of women?

After he discovers Deputy Francis's true identity, Zane asks, "Who would pretend to be a white man in this world? What could be the possible advantage of that?"

In today's culture, do you think it's more believable for a woman to disguise herself as a man, or for a black man to "pass" as white, rather than vice versa? Why?

Artist Warren Pleece updated the original black and white line art with shades of gray for this 10th Anniversary Edition.

Why do you think he chose not to add color to the art?

How do you think this story relates to events in America today?

Mat Johnson is the author of the novels *Loving Day, Pym, Drop*, and *Hunting in Harlem*, the nonfiction novella *The Great Negro Plot*, and the graphic novels *Incognegro* and *Dark Rain*.

He is a recipient of the United States Artist James Baldwin Fellowship, The Hurston-Wright Legacy Award, a Barnes & Noble Discover Great New Writers selection, the John Dos Passos Prize for Literature, and is a regular contributor on NPR's Fresh Air. Mat Johnson is a Professor at the University of Houston Creative Writing Program.

Meera Bowman Johnson

A.Figgs

Warren Pleece is a comic book artist mostly known for his work on DC Comics' Vertigo imprint for titles such as *Deadenders, Hellblazer*, and *Incognegro*. As well as having worked for the magazine *2000AD*, Titan Comics' *Doctor Who* series, and for numerous publishers including Jonathan Cape, Macmillan, and Simon and Shuster, he is also co-creator of a comic magazine, *Velocity*, the graphic novels, *The Great Unwashed* and *Montague Terrace*, and the web series, *Alby Figgs*.

From the creators of *INCOGNEGRO: A GRAPHIC MYSTERY* comes the thrilling prequel...

Set in 1920s New York, Harlem's cub reporter Zane Pinchback goes "incognegro" for the first time to solve the murder of a black writer, found dead at a scandalous interracial party. With the dead writer's cryptic manuscript as his only clue and a mysterious femme fatale as the murder's only witness, Zane finds himself on the hunt through the dark and dangerous streets of "Roaring Twenties" Harlem in search of justice.

A page-turning mini-series of racial divide, ***INCOGNEGRO: RENAISSANCE*** explores segregation, secrets, and self-image as our race-bending protagonist penetrates a world where he feels stranger than ever before.

Coming February 7, 2018

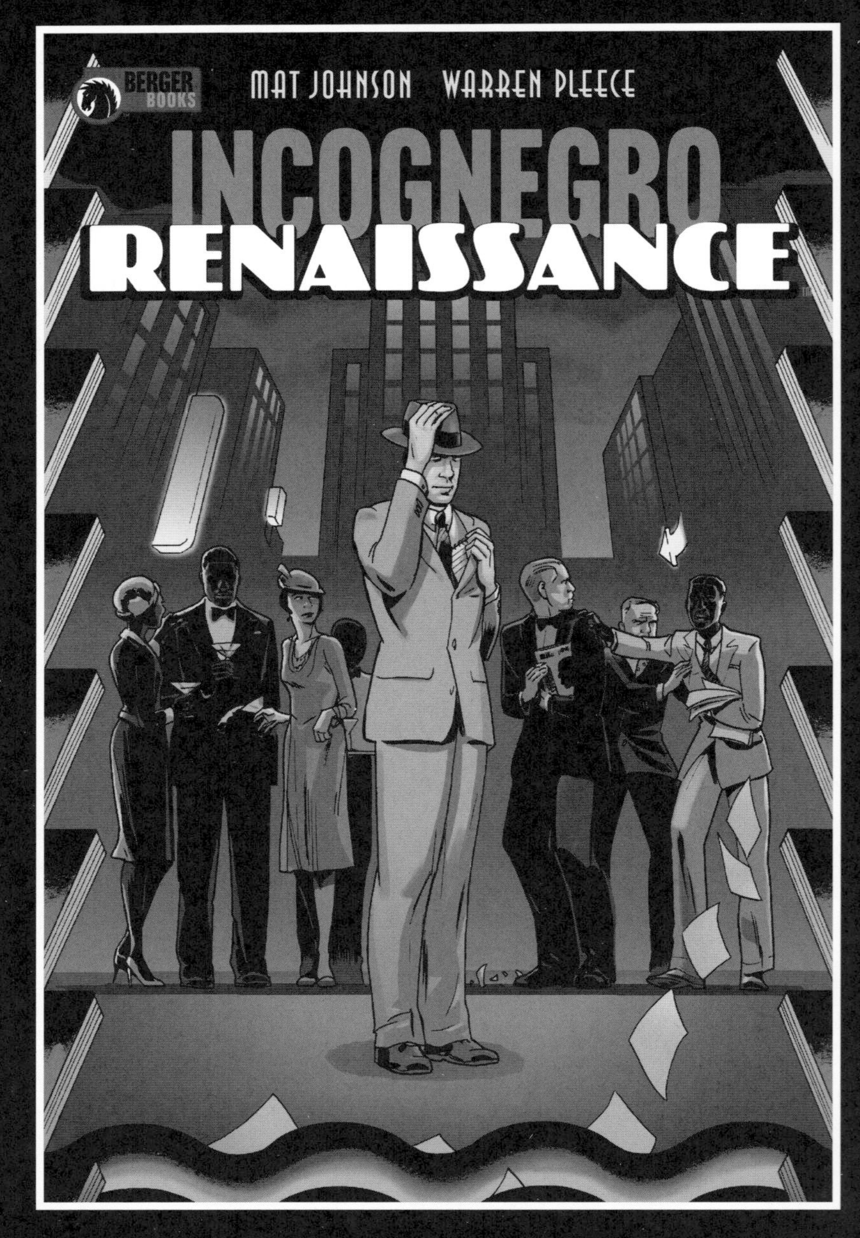

Published by Dark Horse Books, A division of Dark Horse Comics, Inc., 10956 SE Main Street Milwaukie, OR 97222
DarkHorse.com ComicShopLocatorService.com International Licensing: (503) 905-2377